Baudelaire

Jean-Paul Sartre

Baudelaire

Translated from the French by
Martin Turnell

A New Directions Paperbook

New Directions Books are published for James Laughlin by
New Directions Publishing Corporation,
80 Eighth Avenue, New York 10011

NINTH PRINTING

Baudelaire

FOREWORD

'THE READER,' writes M. Sartre towards the end of his essay, 'will have looked in vain for some explanation of the very particular form of Beauty which the poet chose and which makes his poems inimitable. For many people, indeed, Baudelaire is rightly, purely and simply the author of the *Fleurs du mal;* and they regard any form of research as useless which does not increase our appreciation and understanding of Baudelaire's poetry.'

French critics were quick to accept the challenge. Some of them complained that in fact he tells us very little about Baudelaire's poetry; and in a foreword to the second French edition, M. Michel Leiris remarked bluntly that for a person who on his own admission is such a stranger to poetry as M. Sartre to write about Baudelaire at all was a bold undertaking.

The essay was originally written as an introduction to M. Sartre's own selections from Baudelaire's diaries and letters. It will be apparent from the first page that it is an Existentialist study, and it occupies a special place in its author's work. In his purely philosophical writings like *l'Etre et le néant* M. Sartre discusses Man in general terms. The two essays on Descartes are examinations of the Cartesian system from the point of view of a different philosophy. In the novels and plays he invents concrete characters who are endowed with the qualities which he analysed in his philosophical works. In his *Baudelaire* he has attempted something fresh. He has applied the Existentialist analysis to an historical character as revealed primarily in his intimate personal writings.

The results are in many ways surprising, and the reader may feel that the being whose 'portrait' is drawn in M. Sartre's pages is more like one of the characters from *les Chemins de la liberté* than the historic Baudelaire or the Baudelaire of more orthodox biographers. I think that he will also find it stimulating. 'Criticism,' said Baudelaire himself, 'should be partial, passionate and political, that is to say, written from an exclusive point of view but from the point of view which opens up the widest horizons.' We may leave the width of the horizon for the moment and consider the exclusive point of view. When a critic approaches his subject from a dogmatic standpoint, as one feels that M. Sartre does, the 'portrait' which emerges is necessarily partial and incomplete because in spite of the writer's evident 'good faith' rebellious material is bound to be interpreted in a manner which fits in with his general thesis. And there are undoubtedly pages in the present essay which will only convince those who accept M. Sartre's philosophical premises. Yet the exclusive point of view clearly has its compensations. For in so far as a system contains elements of truth, it does isolate aspects of the poet which have previously escaped notice or received insufficient attention. Emphasis and accent may sometimes appear at fault; undue importance may be attached to part of the poet's work, but in the end something new emerges. That is the justification of the critic and, indeed, of all criticism. It is not the critic's business to do 'the common reader's' work for him. His business is to stimulate him to make his own discoveries, to provide fresh insights which will send the reader back to his texts to test their validity. In so far as he is a competent reader he will profit from these insights and relate them to what seems 'true' in his own conception of the poet. Criticism is essentially a collective work which goes on from one age to another. No single critic can tell the whole truth about a great writer or speak with the same sureness all the time, and no age ever has the last word. The critic can only interpret an author in the light of his own age. His successors will add something to his portrait, but they will also remove what no longer appears true. The individual critic therefore can only make a contribution to a portrait which in the nature of things must remain unfinished.

M. Sartre's book is an essay in what he himself has called 'Existential psycho-analysis,' and it possesses the virtues and defects of the psycho-analytical approach.[1] Now psycho-analysis is primarily a method of diagnosing and treating certain mental and nervous disorders, but it differs from ordinary medicine in that it can never be strictly scientific. It depends directly on the personality of the man who employs it. For behind the technique there is always what, for want of a better word, we must call a 'philosophy' or at least philosophical assumptions. For some of its critics the weakness of the Freudian sys-

[1] See *l'Etre et le néant*, pp. 643–63.

tem lies in the fact that it is based on determinism. M. Sartre employs the psycho-analytical technique, but in his case it is based not on determinism but on his own philosophy.

The psycho-analytical critic claims that by examining the peculiarities of a writer's personality he is in a better position to interpret his work, that he can show that particular words, phrases and images have a special significance for the poet. This approach has one very obvious danger. Concentration on the *man* tends to distract us from his *work* or alternatively it treats the work as a mere 'case-book' in the study of a diseased, or supposedly diseased personality. It follows from this that if psycho-analytical criticism is to be of use in the interpretation of poetry, there must be a double movement. The critic moves from the work to the man, but it is essential that he should make the return journey from the man back to the work. It is the merit of M. Sartre's study that though he sometimes uses Baudelaire's poetry to build up a picture of the Existential man engaged in the attempt to achieve 'the impossible synthesis of existence and being,' he does make the return journey more frequently and more effectively than most other psycho-analytical critics. In spite of his disparaging references to 'depth psychology,' he makes liberal use of the Freudian symbols. His study of Baudelaire's sexual peculiarities enables him to present a highly novel interpretation of the poem called *Une nuit que j'étais près d'une affreuse Juive;* his emphasis on Baudelaire's preoccupation with sterility gives us a fresh appreciation of the function of metal and stone in his poetry; and there is a fascinating exegesis of the unfinished drama *l'Ivrogne*. There is also a remarkable interpretation of Baudelaire's 'dandyism' and of the poet's position in the modern world. At this point, however, some readers will feel that M. Sartre's political bias prevents him from taking Baudelaire's 'dandyism' as seriously as it deserves. Baudelaire's terminology and the nineteenth-century décors with which he surrounded his thought have not worn well, but the attempt to create a new intellectual *élite* does seem to offer the only solution to the problem of the artist's position in a world of warring dictatorships.

At the end of the essay we are confronted with a question. Could the lamentable creature who emerges from it, the man who compromised almost every vital principle and surrendered all the key-positions without fighting, really have been one of the greatest European poets of the nineteenth century? Or has M. Sartre misrepresented Baudelaire? Has he left out something vital or is there some other explanation? I do not think that he has misrepresented Baudelaire, or not in a way that affects our judgment of his artistic achievement. It seems to me that we are inclined to apply the wrong standards, that we have used the word 'heroic' too lightly to describe the poet's attitude towards his age. He certainly understood his age better than most of his contemporaries, but this does not mean that he was prepared to defend the artist's position actively against the encroachments of the 'bourgeois.' There was very little of the crusader about the author of the *Fleurs du mal*. That, however, is not the whole story. When writers began to say that art had nothing to do with morality, the public was shocked as it was meant to be. There was no doubt an element of bravado about the theory, but it contains a profound truth. It is not enough to say that a man's moral weaknesses do not necessarily impair his poetry. It is not even sufficient to say that they are often the stuff out of which his poetry is made. We must add that they are often a positive advantage, that the rottener the man the better the poetry. This may be largely a modern phenomenon—it has certainly become commoner during the last hundred and fifty years—but Racine is already a prime example. Baudelaire did little more than follow his lead. The *Fleurs du mal* are amongst the greatest poetry written in the nineteenth century because they record something which happened to human nature as a whole. We knew long before M. Sartre appeared that the core of Baudelaire's poetry was not merely a sense of utter collapse, but of carefully cultivated inner collapse. There is a further point which M. Sartre does not mention, but which the literary critic cannot overlook. There is undoubtedly a parallel—I am not sure whether one should speak of cause and effect—between Baudelaire's moral compromise and his literary compromise. He speaks to us more urgently, more intimately than almost any other modern poet, but this does not alter the fact that more that was perishable, more poetic clichés and more shoddy images, which were the stock-in-trade of the minor writers of the day, went into his poetry than into that of any other poet of comparable stature. There is hardly a poem in the *Fleurs du mal* which does not contain one or two really bad lines.

M. Sartre presents his translators with a difficult task. There will be no wholly satisfactory translation of his work until we have an agreed terminology, and a comparison between the various translations of his work which have so far been made will show how far we are from that. There are two main difficulties—the difficulty of finding English equivalents for a new terminology and the difficulty caused by the fact that he gives a special nuance to commonplace words. 'Essence' and 'existence' are the two most obvious examples of the second difficulty. Another is the word *dépasser* or *dépassement*. The least ambiguous English equivalents are probably 'transcend' or 'act of transcendence,' but in the French text there is a distinction between *transcendance* meaning the transcendence of material Nature in general and *dépassement* meaning the transcendence of a specific A by a specific B. It is impossible to find a completely adequate translation of the words *un dépassement figé*. It means the interruption of the act of transcendence and probably the nearest one can get is 'an unfulfilled transcendence.' I have tried to avoid loading the text with 'Translator's footnotes,' but one or two other special difficulties have been referred to in this way.

I am indebted to Professor Mansell Jones, and to two philosophers, who wish for ecclesiastical reasons to remain anonymous, for their assistance in unravelling the linguistic and other difficulties which occur in the book. For any shortcomings in the English version I am naturally responsible.

M. T.

BAUDELAIRE

'He didn't have the life he deserved.' Baudelaire's life seems at first a magnificent illustration of this comfortable saying. He certainly didn't deserve that mother, that perpetual want, that family council, that rapacious mistress or that syphilis. And what could have been more unjust than his premature end? Yet when we think it over, a doubt rises. If we consider the man himself, it appears that he was not without faults or contradictions. The perverse individual deliberately chose the most banal and the most rigid of moral codes. The refined man of the world went with the lowest harlots. A taste for squalor kept him hanging around Louchette's skinny body, and his love of the *affreuse Juive* anticipated his love of Jeanne Duval. The recluse had a horror of solitude; he never went a yard without a companion and longed for a home and a family. The apostle of effort was an 'aboulic' who was incapable of settling down to regular work. His poetry is full of 'invitations to travel'; he clamoured for escape from his surroundings, dreamed of undiscovered countries, but he hesitated for six months before making up his mind to go to Honfleur; and his one and only voyage seems to have been a long torment. He flaunted his contempt for and even his hatred of the

15

solemn individuals who acted as his guardians, but he never made any real attempts to rid himself of their ministrations and never missed an opportunity of listening to their fatherly admonitions. Was his life really so alien to him? Supposing after all that he did deserve the sort of life he had? Supposing that contrary to the accepted view, men always have the sort of lives they deserve? We must look more closely into the matter.

Baudelaire was six when his father died. He worshipped his mother and was fascinated by her. He was surrounded by every care and comfort; he did not yet realize that he existed as a separate person, but felt that he was united body and soul to his mother in a primitive mystical relationship. He was submerged in the gentle warmth of their mutual love. There was nothing but a home, a family and an incestuous couple. 'I was always living in you,' he wrote to her in later life; 'you belonged to me alone. You were at once an idol and a friend.'

It would be impossible to improve upon his description of the sacred nature of their union. The mother was an idol, the child *consecrated* by her affection for him. Far from feeling that his existence was vague, aimless, superfluous, he thought of himself as *son by divine right*. He was always living in her which meant that he had found a sanctuary. He himself was nothing and did not want to be anything but an emanation of the divinity, a little thought which was always present in her mind. It was precisely because he was completely absorbed in a being who appeared to be a necessary being, to exist as of right, that he was shielded from any feeling of disquiet, that he melted into the absolute and was *justified*.

In November 1828 the mother whom he worshipped remarried. Her second husband was a soldier. Baudelaire was sent to boarding school and it was from this period that his famous 'flaw' dated. On this point Crépet quotes a significant comment of Buisson's:

'Baudelaire was a very delicate soul—sensitive, original, tender—who had been flawed by the shock of his first contact with the world.'[1]

His mother's second marriage was the one event in his life which he simply could not accept. He was inexhaustible on the subject, and his terrible logic always summed it up in these words:

'When one has a son like me'—'like me' was understood—'one doesn't remarry.'

The sudden break and the grief it caused forced him into a personal existence without any warning or preparation. One moment he was still enveloped in the communal religious life of the couple consisting of his mother and himself; the next life had gone out like a tide leaving him high and dry. The justification for his existence had disappeared; he made the mortifying discovery that he was a single person, that his life had been given him for nothing. His rage at being driven out was colored by a profound sense of having fallen from grace. When later on he thought of this moment, he wrote in *Mon coeur mis à nu:* 'Sense of solitude from childhood. In spite of the family—and above all when surrounded by

[1] E. Crépet, *Charles Baudelaire*, Paris, 1906, p. 11.

children of my own age—I had a sense of being destined to eternal solitude.' He already thought of his isolation as a *destiny*. That meant that he did not accept it passively. On the contrary, he embraced it with fury, shut himself up in it and, since he was condemned to it, hoped that at any rate his condemnation was final. This brings us to the point at which Baudelaire chose the sort of person he would be—that irrevocable choice by which each of us decides in a particular situation what he will be and what he is. When he found himself abandoned and rejected, Baudelaire chose solitude deliberately as an act of self-assertion, so that his solitude should not be something inflicted on him by other people. The abrupt revelation of his individual existence made him *feel* that he was *another person;* but at the same time and in a mood of humiliation, rancor and pride, he asserted this otherness of his own accord. From this moment, he set to work with an obstinate, painful fury to *make* himself another person, to make himself into someone different from his mother, with whom he had been identical and who had rejected him; someone different from his coarse, carefree companions. He felt and was determined to feel that he was unique; and he pushed this sense of uniqueness to the point of extreme solitary enjoyment and of terror.

But his sense of abandonment and isolation was not balanced by anything positive, by the discovery of some special virtue which would at once have placed him beyond comparison with other people. The white blackbird, who is spurned by all the black blackbirds, at least has the consolation of looking out of the corner of its eye at the whiteness of its wings. Men are never white blackbirds. What the abandoned child experiences is a feeling of otherness which is purely formal; his experience is not even sufficient to distinguish him from other people. Each of us was able to observe in childhood the fortuitous and shattering advent of self-consciousness. Gide has described the experience in *Si le grain ne meurt* and after him Mme. Maria Le Hardouin in *la Voile noire;* but no one has described it better than Hughes in *A High Wind in Jamaica:*

'Emily had been playing in a nook right in the bows . . . and tiring of it was walking rather aimlessly aft . . . when it suddenly flashed into her mind that she was *she.* . . . Once fully convinced of this astonishing fact, that she was now Emily Bas-Thornton . . . she began seriously to reckon its implications. . . . What agency had so ordered it that out of all the people in the world who she might have been, she was this particular one, this Emily: born in such-and-such a year out of all the years in Time. . . . Had she chosen herself, or had God done it? . . . Wasn't she perhaps God, herself? . . . There was her family, a number of brothers and sisters from whom, before, she had never entirely dissociated herself; but now she got such a sudden feeling of being a distinct person that they seemed as separate from her as the ship itself. . . . A sudden terror struck her: did anyone know? (Know, I mean, that she was someone in particular, Emily—perhaps even God—not just any little girl.) She could not tell why, but the idea terrified her. . . . At all costs she must hide *that* from them.'[2]

This lightning intuition is completely empty. The child has just acquired the conviction that she is not just anyone, but it is precisely by acquiring this conviction that she becomes just anyone. She feels, to be sure, that she is someone different from the others, but each of the others has the same feeling of being different from everyone else. The child has undergone a purely negative experience of separation and her experience assumes the form of universal subjectivism—a sterile form which Hegel defined by the equation $I=I$. What can we make of a discovery which frightens us and offers nothing in return? Most people contrive to forget it as quickly as possible. But the child who has become aware of himself as a separate being with a sense of despair, rage and jealousy will base his whole life on the fruitless contemplation of a singularity which is formal. 'You threw me out,' he will say to his parents. 'You threw me out of the perfect whole of which I was part and condemned me to a separate existence. Well, now I'm going to turn this existence against you. If you ever wanted to get me back again, it would be impossible because I have become conscious of myself as separate from and against everybody else.' And he will say to his school-fellows and the street urchins who persecute him: 'I'm someone else, someone different from all of you who are responsible for my sufferings. You can persecute my body, but you can't touch my "otherness."' This assertion is both

[2] *A High Wind in Jamaica*, London, 1929, pp. 134, 136, 138–9.

a claim and a gesture of defiance. He is someone else, and because he is someone else he is out of reach and already almost revenged on his oppressors. He prefers himself to everyone else because everyone else abandons him. His preference for himself is primarily a defense-mechanism, but it is also in a sense an *ascesis* because for the child it takes the form of pure self-consciousness. It is an heroic, an aggressive choice of the abstract, a desperate stripping of oneself, at once an act of renunciation and affirmation. It has a name and its name is pride. It is a stoic pride, a metaphysical pride which owes nothing to social distinctions, to success or to any recognized form of superiority or indeed to anything at all in this world. It simply appears as an absolute event, an *a priori* choice which is entirely unmotivated and belongs to a sphere far above any of those where failure could destroy or success sustain it.

This form of pride is as unhappy as it is pure because it revolves in the void and feeds upon itself. It is always unsatisfied, always exasperated and exhausts itself in the very act of asserting itself. It is founded on nothing; it is entirely in the air because the sense of being different, which creates it, is an empty concept that is universal. Yet the child wants to enjoy his sense of being different from other people; he wants to *feel* that he is different from his brother in the same way that he feels his brother is different from his father. He dreams of a uniqueness which is perceptible to sight and touch and which fills us as pure sound fills the ears. His purely formal difference seems to him to be the symbol of a deeper singularity which is identical with what he *is*. He bends over himself and tries to discover his own image in the calm, grey river which always flows at the same speed. He gazes at his desires and his fits of anger in the hope of discovering the secret of his own nature. It is through this undivided attention to his own moods that he gradually becomes the man whom we call Charles Baudelaire.

Baudelaire's fundamental attitude was that of a man bending over himself—bending over his own reflection like Narcissus. With Baudelaire there was no immediate consciousness which was not pierced by his steely gaze. For the rest of us it is enough to see the tree or the house; we forget ourselves, completely absorbed in contemplation of them. Baudelaire was the man who never forgot himself. He watched himself see; he watched in order to see himself watch; it was his own consciousness of the tree and the house that he contemplated. He only saw things through this consciousness; they were paler, smaller and less touching as though seen through an eye-glass. They did not point to one another as a signpost points the way or a marker indicates the page, and Baudelaire's mind never became lost in their intricacies. On the contrary, their immediate function was to direct awareness back to the self. 'What does it matter,' he wrote, 'what the reality outside me is made of provided that it helps me to feel that I am and what I am?' In his own art his one concern was to show things only as they appeared through a layer of human consciousness. For in *l'Art philosophique* he wrote:

'What is the modern conception of pure art? It is to create a suggestive magic which contains both subject and object, the external world and the artist himself.' [3]

Since this was his view, he might very well have written a *Treatise on the Unreality of the External World*. Objects were pretexts, reflections, screens, but they were never of any value in themselves; their only purpose was to give him an opportunity of contemplating himself while he was looking at them.

The basic distance between Baudelaire and the world was not the same as ours. In his case we are aware of something translucent, slightly damp and rather too highly perfumed, which insinuated itself between the man and his object like the vibration of the warm air in summer. This consciousness which was watched and scrutinized and which knew that it was being watched and scrutinized while it performed its normal functions, at once lost its naturalness like a child playing under the eyes of grown-up people. Baudelaire possessed nothing of this 'naturalness' which he so hated and regretted. Everything was faked because everything was scrutinized and because the slightest mood or the feeblest desire was *observed* and *unravelled* at the very moment it came into being. We have only to recall the meaning which Hegel gave to the word 'immediate' to realize that Baudelaire's profound singularity lay in the fact that he was the man without 'immediacy.'

But if his singularity is valid *for us* who see him from outside, it completely eluded Baudelaire who saw him-

[3] In *l'Art romantique,* Ed. J. Crépet (Conard) p. 119. (In the absence of a contrary indication, all references are to the Conard edition. *Tr.*)

self from within. He was trying to discover his own *nature,* that is to say, his character and his being, but all he saw was the long, monotonous procession of his states of mind. He grew exasperated. He perceived so clearly what constituted the singularity of General Aupick or of his mother. Why then should he be deprived of the private enjoyment of his own originality? Because he was the victim of the very natural illusion that the outer man is modelled on the inner man. That is not true. There was not a word in the language of the inner man which could describe the distinctive quality which attracted the attention of other people. He himself did not feel or know this quality. Could he *feel* that he was spiritual or vulgar or distinguished? Could he even measure the breadth and vivacity of his own intelligence? His intelligence had no limit beyond itself; and except when some drug heightened the tempo of his thoughts for a moment, so used was he to their rhythm and so completely lacking in any terms of comparison, that he was incapable of appreciating the speed at which they moved. As for the details of his ideas and affections, which were sensed and recognized before they had even appeared and became transparent through and through, they gave him the impression of something 'already seen,' something that he 'knew too well.' They had about them a sort of colorless familiarity, a flavor of something remembered. He was full of himself to overflowing, but this 'self' was nothing but a vapid, glassy mood without consistency or resistance which he could neither judge nor observe, which had neither light nor shade—a garrulous consciousness which declared that it was itself in an unending murmur which could never be quickened. He stuck too closely to himself to be able to guide himself or even to get a proper view of himself; but he saw too much of himself to get completely bogged and lost in a mute adhesion to his own life.

It was at this point that the drama of Baudelaire began. Imagine for a moment that the white blackbird has gone blind—for too great a volume of reflective light is the same as blindness. He is haunted by the idea of a certain whiteness spreading out over his wings which all the blackbirds see and discuss with him, but which he alone is unable to see. Baudelaire's famous lucidity was nothing but an attempt at *recovery*.[4] The problem was to recover *himself* and—as sight is a form of appropriation—to see *himself*. But he could only have seen *himself* if he had been two people. He could see his hands and his arms because the eye and the hand are separate; but the eye cannot see itself. It feels itself and is aware

[4] In French, *récupération*. The words, 'recovery' and 'recover' occur frequently in the pages which follow. They are an example of the way in which M. Sartre gives a special philosophical overtone to common words. The idea of 'recovery' appears to follow from his view of the nature and structure of consciousness. He believes that we can never have possession of it 'like a thing.' If this is so, there can, strictly speaking, be no question of *re*covering it; but the prefix probably contains an implicit reference to the derivation of consciousness (*le pour-soi*) from non-consciousness (*l'en-soi*) which is self-identical being. According to M. Sartre, man strives (*though in vain*) to ground himself as conscious, to become completely self-possessed consciousness, absolute consciousness. Although this striving is vain, '*re*covery' may refer to the 'fact' that consciousness is secondary and derived and that man tries to 'recover' on the plane of consciousness what he has lost on the plane of 'being.' *Tr.*

that it is alive; but it cannot place itself at the necessary distance from itself to see itself. It was in vain that Baudelaire exclaimed in the *Fleurs du mal*:

> *Tête-à-tête sombre et limpide*
> *Qu'un coeur devenu son miroir!*

The 'tête-à-tête' had scarcely begun before it was broken off. There was only one 'head.' The whole of Baudelaire's efforts were devoted to pushing to its last extreme this abortive duality which we call the reflective consciousness. If he was lucid from the first, it was not in order to make an exact inventory of his faults; it was *in order to be two people*. If he wanted to be two people, it was in order to realize in this couple the final possession of the Self by the Self. This meant that he exasperated his own lucidity. He was simply his own witness; he tried to become his own executioner, tried to become the *Heautontimoroumenos*. For torture brings into existence a closely united couple in which the executioner *appropriates* the victim. Because he did not succeed in his attempt to see *himself*, Baudelaire made up his mind that at any rate he would explore himself as the knife explores the wound in the hope of reaching the 'lonely depths' which constituted his true nature:

> *Je suis la plaie et le couteau*
> *Et la victime et le bourreau.*

Thus the tortures which he inflicted on himself simulated possession. They tended to make flesh—his own flesh—grow beneath his fingers so that in the very throes of its sufferings it would recognize that it was his flesh. To cause suffering was just as much a form of possession and creation as destruction. The link between the victim and the inquisitor was sexual, but Baudelaire tried to transfer into his inner life a relationship which could only have had any meaning if it had existed between two separate persons. He attempted to make the reflective consciousness into the knife and the reflected consciousness into the wound. In a way they are identical. You cannot love, hate or torture yourself on your own. Victim and executioner disappear in a general blur when by a single voluntary act one demands and the other inflicts pain. By a reverse movement, which was nevertheless directed towards the same end, Baudelaire slyly tried to make himself the accomplice of his reflected consciousness against his reflective consciousness. When he stopped torturing himself, it was because he was trying to take himself by surprise. He simulated a disconcerting spontaneity, pretended to surrender to the most gratuitous impulses so that he could suddenly appear in his own eyes as an opaque, unpredictable object, appear in fact as though he were *Another Person*. If he had succeeded in this, his task would have been more than half accomplished; he would have been able to derive enjoyment from himself. But here again he was identical with the person whom he wished to surprise. It would be an understatement to say that he divined his own plan before it was conceived; he foresaw and measured his own astonishment or, if one may say so, ran after his astonishment without ever catching up with it. Baudelaire was the man who chose to look upon himself as though he were another person; his life is simply the story of the failure of this attempt.

For in spite of tricks which we shall presently describe and which created the image which we shall always have of him, he knew very well that his famous look was identical with the thing at which he was looking, that he would never attain true possession of himself, but simply that listless sampling of himself which is characteristic of reflective knowledge. He was bored and the *ennui* which he described as 'the bizarre affliction which was the source of all [his] ills and all [his] miserable progress,'[5] was not an accident nor, as he sometimes claimed, the fruit of his blasé *incuriosité*. It was the *pur ennui* of which Valéry has spoken; it was the taste which man necessarily possesses for himself, the savor of his existence:

> *Je suis un vieux boudoir plein de roses fanées*
> *Où gît tout un fouillis de modes surannées*
> *Où les pastels plaintifs et les pâles Boucher,*
> *Seuls, respirent l'odeur d'un parfum débouché.*

This stale yet obsessive perfume, scarcely noticed but gently and terribly present, which drifts out of the uncorked bottle, is the most effective symbol of the existence *for-itself* of consciousness. Baudelaire's *ennui* was therefore a metaphysical feeling, was his interior landscape and the material out of which he fashioned his joys, his furies and his sufferings. This brings us to a fresh misfortune. He was obsessed by the intuition of his formal singularity only to realize that it was an at-

[5] *Petits poèms en prose:* 'le Joueur généreux,' p. 105.

tribute which belonged to every one. In other words, he had embarked on the way of lucidity in order to discover his own singular nature and the various attributes which together would have made him the most irreplaceable of beings; yet what he actually discovered on the way was not his own particular face, but the indeterminate modes of the universal consciousness. Pride, lucidity and *ennui* were identical; in him and in spite of himself it was the consciousness of everybody which met and recognized itself.

Now this consciousness saw itself first of all as something completely gratuitous which had neither cause nor end, as something uncreated and unjustifiable whose only claim to existence was the mere fact that it already existed. It could not find outside itself any pretext, any excuse or any *raison d'être* because nothing could exist for it unless it first took cognizance of it and because nothing had any meaning except the meaning which consciousness gave it. This accounts for Baudelaire's profound sense of his own uselessness. We shall see a little later that his obsession with suicide was a means of protecting his life rather than of putting an end to it; but if he often thought of suicide it was because as a man he felt that he was superfluous.

'I am going to kill myself,' he said in the famous letter written in 1845, 'because I am useless to other people and a danger to myself.' [6]

[6] *Correspondance générale,* 1, p. 71. (Since the publication of M. Sartre's essay, the first two volumes of Baudelaire's letters have been added by M. Jacques Crépet to the Conard edition. They contain all existing letters written from 1833 to 1859. *Tr.*)

It must not be supposed that he felt useless because he was a young bourgeois without a profession who at the age of twenty-four was still supported by his family. On the contrary, if he did not take up a profession, if he refused in advance to show the slightest interest in every form of business, it was because he had already made up his mind that he was completely useless. At a later date he wrote, proudly this time: 'To be a useful man has always appeared to me to be something particularly hideous.' The contradiction came from his sudden changes of mood. Whether he boasted about it or blamed himself for it, the one thing which counted for him was constant and, as it were, his basic detachment. The man who wants to make himself useful chooses the opposite direction to Baudelaire. He moves from the world to consciousness; he takes up his stand on a number of well-defined moral or political principles which he regards as absolute and to which he begins by submitting. He simply considers himself, body and soul, as a certain thing in the middle of other things—a thing which is subject to rules which it has not discovered on its own account and which are the means of realizing a particular order. But if you have begun by sampling to the point of nausea this consciousness, which has neither rhyme nor reason and which has to invent the rules which it proposes to obey, usefulness ceases to have any meaning at all. Life is nothing more than a game; man has to choose his own end without waiting for orders, notice or advice. Once a man has grasped this truth—that there is no other end in this life except the one that he has deliberately chosen, he no longer feels any great desire to look for one.

'Life,' wrote Baudelaire, 'has only one real attraction —the attraction of a *gamble*. But supposing that it is a matter of indifference to us whether we can win or lose?' If we are to believe in an enterprise we need in the first place to be pitched into it; we have to ask ourselves what is the best method of bringing it to a successful conclusion; we must not ask ourselves what its object is. For a thoughtful person every enterprise is absurd. Baudelaire steeped himself in this sense of absurdity. Suddenly for a trifle, a mere feeling of disappointment or tiredness, he discovered the unending solitude of this consciousness which was 'as vast as the sea' and which was at one and the same time *the* general consciousness and *his* consciousness. He realized that he was incapable of finding any signposts, any support or any orders outside it. He therefore allowed himself to *drift*, buffeted by the monotonous waves. It was when he was in one of these moods that he wrote to his mother:

'. . . what I feel is an immense discouragement, a sense of unbearable isolation . . . a complete absence of desires, an impossibility of finding any sort of amusement. The strange success of my book and the hatred it aroused interested me for a short time, but after that I sank back into my usual mood.' [7]

He himself described it as his laziness. I agree that it has a pathological aspect. I also agree that it bears a

[7] Letter of December 30th, 1857. (*Corres. gén.*, 2, p. 108.)

strong resemblance to those disorders which Janet has described collectively as neurasthenia. It must not be forgotten, however, that as a result of their condition, Janet's patients frequently had metaphysical intuitions which the normal person tries to hide from himself. The motive and meaning of his laziness were that Baudelaire could not 'take' his enterprises 'seriously.' He realized only too well that one only found in them what one had oneself begun by putting into them.

Still, one had to act. If on the one hand he was the knife, the pure contemplative look which saw the hurrying waves of the reflected consciousness unfold beneath it, he was also and at the same time the wound, the actual consequence of those waves. If for him the plane of reflection was in itself a disgust with action, underneath it he was through each of these ephemeral little consciousnesses which he reflected, act, project, hope. For this reason we must not regard him as a quietist, but rather as an infinite series of spontaneous enterprises (which were immediately disarmed by the reflective look like a sea of projects which broke the moment they appeared), as a continual waiting, a perpetual desire to be someone else and somewhere else. I am not speaking here only of the innumerable expedients by which he tried hastily and nervously to put off the crash, to extort a few ha'pence from his mother or an advance from Ancelle, but also of the various literary plans which he carried around with him for twenty years—plays, criticism, *Mon coeur mis à nu*—without ever managing to finish them. The form taken by his laziness was sometimes a torpor, but more often a feverish, sterile agitation which knew that it was vain and which was poisoned by a merciless lucidity. He appears in his letters like an ant which is determined to climb up a wall, falls every time and then starts all over again. For no one understood the futility of his efforts better than himself. If he did act, it was, as he himself said, like an explosion, a shock, when he managed for a moment to escape from his own lucidity.

'There are natures which are purely contemplative and completely unadapted to action which nevertheless under a mysterious unknown impulse sometimes act with a rapidity of which they would have believed themselves incapable. . . . There comes a moment when (these souls), who are incapable of carrying out the simplest and most necessary actions, display a sort of *de luxe* courage in executing the most absurd and often indeed the most dangerous exploits.' [8]

He actually described these sudden acts as *actes gratuits*. They were frankly useless and often assumed a destructive character. They also had to be carried out quickly before the return of the look which poisoned everything. This explains the hurried, imperious note of some of the letters to his mother:

'I must move quickly, so quickly!'

There is a furious outburst against Ancelle. Baudelaire's rage is terrible. He writes five letters to his mother

[8] *Petits poèmes en prose:* 'Le Mauvais Vitrier,' pp. 21–2.

on the same day and a sixth the following morning. In the first he speaks of nothing less than slapping Ancelle's face:

> 'Ancelle is a wretch. I am going to SLAP HIS FACE IN FRONT OF his wife and CHILDREN. I AM GOING TO SLAP HIS FACE at four o'clock (it's now half past two).'[9]

The capitals are used as though to engrave his resolution on marble, so afraid is he that it may slip through his fingers. His plans are such short-term plans, he distrusts tomorrow so strongly that he fixes a zero hour for carrying them out: four o'clock. He will just have time to rush to Neuilly. But at four o'clock he dispatches a fresh note:

> 'I shan't go to Neuilly today. I am prepared to wait until tomorrow for my revenge.'[10]

The plan remains, but it is already neutralized, has already become conditional:

> 'If he doesn't make *exemplary amends,* I shall hit Ancelle. I shall hit his son . . .'[11]

All the same, he only mentions it in a postscript, probably because he was afraid of appearing to give in too easily. During the evening, there is a further weakening of his determination:

> 'I've already discussed what I'm going to do with two other people. It's a very horrible thing to hit an

[9] *Corres. gén.,* 2, p. 152.   [10] *ibid.,* p. 153.   [11] *ibid.,* p. 153.

old man in front of his family. Yet I must have my apology;—what should I do if I didn't get it;—I must—at least—go and tell him in front of his wife and children what I think of his behavior.' [12]

The need for action already seems too heavy a burden. A few moments ago he wanted to frighten his mother, blackmail her by threats of violence; he must have an exemplary apology on the spot. Now he is terrified to death that the apology may not take place because if it didn't he would have to act. Already he is bored with the whole affair; he writes at the end of the passage I have just quoted:

'Lord, in what a difficult position you've put me! I simply must have a little rest. I ask nothing more than that.' [13]

On the Sunday morning there is no longer any question of apology or reparation:

'*I mustn't write to him again at all,* except a line to say that I no longer need his money.' [14]

All that he wants is silence, oblivion, a symbolical annihilation of Ancelle. He talks again of revenging himself, but in a vague way at some time in the remote future. Nine days later the whole incident is closed:

'Yesterday's letter to Ancelle was correct. The reconciliation was correct.
'He had come here while I was on the way to see

[12] *ibid.*, p. 158.   [13] *ibid.*, p. 158.   [14] *ibid.*, p. 160.

him. I am so weary of all this bickering that I didn't even want the bother of making sure that he hadn't come to lecture this Danneval.

'Ancelle told me that he was categorically denying *most* of the remarks.

'Naturally I don't want to have to put his word against a tradesman's. Taken all round, he still has a fault which he'll never get over—his childish, provincial curiosity and the easy-going way in which he gossips with all and sundry.' [15]

Such was the rhythm of action in Baudelaire: an exaggerated violence in conception as though this were necessary to give him the strength to act; sudden explosiveness at the beginning of the operation—then, suddenly, his lucidity returned: What's the good of it? He turned away from his own plan of action which rapidly disintegrated. For his basic attitude prevented him from carrying out any lengthy undertaking. Thus his life gives the impression of being a series of jerks and clashes and, at the same time, of being monotonous. It was a perpetual fresh start which invariably ended in frustration seen against a background of dreary indifference; and if he had not dated his letters to his mother they would be very difficult to arrange in chronological order because they are all so alike. But whether they happened to be immediate actions or continuing enterprises, these plans, which he could never carry out, were always before his eyes. They forced themselves on his attention unceasingly, urgently, helplessly. If he suppressed completely

[15] *ibid.*, pp. 184–5.

the spontaneity of the reflected consciousness, by doing so he arrived at an even better understanding of its nature. He knew that it was its nature to hurl itself outside itself, to transcend itself in order to attain an end. That is why he was, perhaps, the first to define man by what lay beyond him.

'Alas! man's vices . . . contain the proof (even if it were only on account of their infinite expansion) of his thirst for the infinite; only it is a thirst which often mistakes its way. . . . It seems to me that the depravity of man's sense of the infinite is the source of all his criminal excesses . . .' [16]

For Baudelaire, the infinite was not a vast given limitless expanse, though he did sometimes use the word in this sense. It was in fact something which never finished and could not finish. For example, a series of numerals will be infinite not because there is a very large number of them which we can describe as an 'infinite' number, but because of the everlasting possibility of adding another unit to a number however large it may be. Thus every number in the series has a 'beyond' in relation to which it is defined and its place in the series fixed. But this 'beyond' does not yet exist completely: I must bring it into existence by adding another unit to the number in front of me. It already gives meaning to all the other numerals which I have written down, yet it is the term of an operation which I have still not completed. Such was Baudelaire's conception of infinity. It is something which is, without being given; something which today defines me

[16] *Les Paradis artificiels*, p. 6.

and which nevertheless will not exist until tomorrow. It is the term—a term of which we catch a glimpse, dream of and almost touch but which remains out of reach— of a directed movement. We shall see later on that more than to any other, Baudelaire clung to these suggested existences which were present and absent at the same time. But it is certain that he had long recognized that this infinitude was the lot of consciousness. In *l'Invitation au voyage* in the *Petits poèmes en prose,* he wants 'to dream, to prolong the hours by the infinity of sensations.' In *le Confiteor* he writes: 'There are certain delicious sensations whose vagueness does not exclude intensity: there is no sharper point than that of infinity.' We shall return to this determination of the present by the future, of what already exists by what does not yet exist which he called 'non-satisfaction' (*insatisfaction*) and which philosophers today call transcendence. No one understood better than he that man is 'a being of distances'[17] who is defined much more by his end and the terms of his plans than by what we can know of him if we limit him to the passing moment:

'There are in every man at every moment two simultaneous postulations, one towards God, the other towards Satan.

'The invocation to God or spirituality is a desire to mount in the scale; that of Satan or animality is a joy in going downwards.'

Thus man is revealed as a tension which results from the application of two opposing forces; and at bottom

[17] Heidegger, *Vom Wesen des Grundes.*

38

each of these two forces aims at the destruction of the human element because one tries to turn him into an angel and the other into an animal. When Pascal wrote that 'man is neither angel nor beast,' he regarded him as a sort of unchanging state, an intermediate 'nature.' There is nothing of the sort here. According to Baudelaire's conception, man is not a 'state'; he is the clash of two opposing movements which are both centrifugal and of which one is directed upwards and the other downwards. They are movements without driving power, mere spouts—two forms of transcendence which, to borrow a distinction of Jean Wahl's, we might call *transascendance* and *transdescendance*.[18] For man's brutishness like his angelicism must be understood in the strongest sense of the term. It is not simply a question of the all-too-celebrated weakness of the flesh or the all-powerfulness of the lower instincts; Baudelaire was not wrapping up a moralist's sermon in a picturesque image. He believed in Magic and the 'postulation towards Satan' seemed to him to be a piece of sorcery which was similar to that of primitive peoples who put on a bear's skin, dance the bears' dance and 'turn into bears.' He has expressed himself very clearly on the point in *Fusées:*

'Minette, minoutte, minouille, my little cat, my wolf, my little monkey, big monkey, big snake, my melancholy little donkey.

'Such tricks of the tongue when repeated too often or animal names which are used too frequently point

[18] There are no English equivalents. The words mean to transcend in an upwards and downwards direction respectively. *Tr.*

to a Satanic element in love. Don't devils assume animal forms? Cazotte's camel—camel, devil and woman.'

This perception of our own transcendence and of our unjustifiable gratuitousness must at the same time be a revelation of human freedom. And in fact Baudelaire always felt that he was free. We shall see later what tricks he employed to hide his freedom from himself; but from one end of his work and his correspondence to the other this freedom is affirmed, bursts out in spite of himself. There is no doubt that, for reasons which we have already mentioned, he did not possess the great freedom which is the usual attribute of creative power, but he constantly felt an explosive unpredictability which nothing could hem in. He redoubled his precautions against it, but in vain. He noted down in capital letters in his papers 'the little practical maxims, rules, imperatives, acts of faith and formulas which pre-judge the future.'[19] It was still in vain. He eluded himself; he knew that he could hold on to nothing. If only he could have felt that he was partly a machine, it would have been possible to discover the lever which stopped it, altered its course or accelerated it. Determinism is reassuring. Anyone who knows things by their causes can base his actions on causation; and up to the present the moralists have spent their time trying to persuade us that we are machines which can be regulated by easy means. Baudelaire knew that springs and levers had nothing to do with his case; he was neither cause nor effort. He was free

[19] Blin, *Baudelaire*, Paris, 1939, p. 49.

which meant that he could look for no help either inside or outside himself against his own freedom. He bent over it and became giddy at the sight of the gulf:

'Morally and physically I have always been haunted by the sensation of the gulf, not merely the gulf of sleep, but the gulf of action, dreams, memories, desires, regrets, remorse, the beautiful, numbers, etc. . . .'

In another place he wrote:

'Now I always feel giddy.'

Baudelaire was the man who felt that he was a gulf. Pride, *ennui,* giddiness—he looked right into the bottom of his heart. He saw that he was incomparable, incommunicable, uncreated, absurd, useless, abandoned in the most complete isolation, bearing his burden alone, condemned to justify his existence all alone, and endlessly eluding himself, slipping through his own fingers, withdrawn in contemplation and, at the same time, dragged out of himself in an unending pursuit, a bottomless gulf without walls and without darkness, a mystery in broad daylight, unpredictable yet perfectly known. It was his misfortune that his image still eluded him. He was looking for the reflection of a certain Charles Baudelaire, the son of Mme. Aupick—the General's wife—a poet who had got into debt and the lover of the negress Duval. His gaze encountered the human condition itself. His freedom, his gratuitousness and his abandonment which frightened him were the lot of humanity; they did not belong particularly to him. Could one ever touch *one-*

self, see *oneself?* Perhaps this singular unchanging essence was only visible to others. Perhaps it was absolutely necessary to be outside in order to see its characteristics. Perhaps one didn't *exist* for oneself in the manner of an object. Perhaps one didn't *exist* at all. If one were always a question mark, always in suspense, perhaps one would be perpetually obliged to *form* oneself. The whole of Baudelaire's efforts were devoted to hiding these unpleasant thoughts from himself. And since his 'nature' escaped him, he tried to seize it in other people's eyes. His good faith abandoned him; he had to try unceasingly to convince himself, to seize himself with his own eyes. In our eyes—but not in his own—a fresh trait appears: he was the man who felt most deeply his condition as man, but who tried most passionately to hide it from himself.

Because he chose lucidity, because he discovered in spite of himself the gratuitousness, the abandonment, the redoubtable freedom of consciousness, Baudelaire was faced with an alternative—since there were no ready-made principles on which he could rely for support, he either had to stagnate in a state of amoral indifference or himself invent Good and Evil. Because the conscious self [20] derives its laws from itself, it must regard itself in Kant's words as the legislator of the city of ends. It must accept complete responsibility and create its own values, must give meaning to the world and to its own life. In-

[20] In French, *conscience*. The French word is notoriously ambiguous. It normally means either 'conscience' or 'consciousness' according to the context. In spite of the reference to Kant, neither word is a satisfactory translation in this paragraph and I have therefore translated it as 'the conscious self.' *Tr.*

deed, the man who declared that 'what is created by the spirit is more alive than matter' had felt more keenly than most other men the power and mission of the conscious self. He had seen very clearly that with the conscious self something comes into being which did not exist before—meaning. It therefore led to perpetual creation at all levels. Baudelaire attached such price to this creation out of nothing, which for him was characteristic of the *spirit,* that the purely contemplative tonelessness of his life was shot through and through by a creative *élan.* This misanthrope subscribed to a humanism based on creation. He admitted that there were 'three sorts of beings who are respectable: the priest, the warrior and the poet. Knowledge, killing and creation.' It will be seen that in this passage destruction and creation form a pair. In both cases there is the production of absolute events; in both a man is responsible alone for a radical change in the universe. This pair is opposed by knowledge which takes us back to the contemplative life. It would be impossible to demonstrate more clearly the complementary nature of the link which for Baudelaire always united the magic powers of the spirit to his own passive lucidity. He defined the human by its power of creation, not by its power of action. Action implies determinism; its efficacity forms part of the chain of cause and effect; it obeys nature in order to obtain command of nature; it submits to principles which it has taken over blindly without questioning their validity. The man of action is the person who interrogates himself about means, but never about ends. No one was farther from action than Baudelaire. At the end of the passage we have just quoted he added: 'Other men are talliable and liable to forced labor, are made for the stable, that is to say, for carrying on what is known as a *profession*.' But creation is pure freedom; before it there is nothing; it begins by creating its own principles. First and foremost it invents its own end and in that way it partakes of the gratuitousness of consciousness. It is a gratuitousness which is willed, thought out and erected into a goal. This explains in part Baudelaire's love of artifice. In his eyes cosmetics, finery and clothes were a sign of the true greatness of man—his creative power. We know that after Rétif, Balzac and Sue, he contributed very largely to the spread of what Roger Caillois calls 'the myth of the great city.' A city is a perpetual creation: its buildings, smells, sounds and traffic belong to the human kingdom. Everything in it is *poetry* in the strict sense of the term. It is in this sense that the electrically operated advertisements, neon lights and cars which about the year 1920 roused the wonder of young people were profoundly Baudelairean. The great city is a reflection of the gulf which is human freedom. And Baudelaire, who hated man and 'the tyranny of the human face,' discovered that he was after all a humanist because of his cult of the works of man.

Since this is so a lucid consciousness, which above everything else is in love with its demonic powers, owes it to itself to create first the meaning which will illuminate the whole world for it. Absolute creation—the creation of which all other forms are simply a consequence—is the creation of a scale of values. We should therefore have expected Baudelaire to display the boldness of a Nietzsche in the pursuit of Good and Evil—of *his* Good and *his* Evil. Now anyone who examines the life and. works of the poet at all closely is struck by the fact that all his ideas of morality were derived from other people and that he never questioned them. This would be understandable if Baudelaire had assumed an attitude of indifference, an easy-going Epicureanism. But the moral principles which he retained and which were inculcated by a middle-class Catholic education were not in his case mere survivals, mere useless withered organs. Baudelaire possessed an intense moral life; he twisted and turned in his remorse; every day he exhorted himself to do better; he struggled and succumbed; he was overwhelmed by a horrible sense of guilt, so much so that people have wondered whether he was not weighed down by the burden of some secret crime. In his biographical introduction to the *Fleurs du mal,* M. Crépet remarks very justly:

> 'Was there some crime in his life which time does not obliterate? It is difficult to believe after all the inquests to which it has been subjected. Yet he treats himself as a criminal and declares that he is guilty "on all counts." He denounces himself on the ground that though he possesses a sense of duty and all the moral obligations, he always betrays them' (p. xxxviii).

No, Baudelaire was not burdened with some secret crime. The crimes which can be imputed to him are not capital ones: a dryness of heart which was real enough but not total, a certain laziness, abuse of narcotics, probably some sexual peculiarities and a certain lack of scruple which sometimes bordered on fraud. If he had only once made up his mind to challenge the principles in the name of which he was condemned by General Aupick and Ancelle he would have been free. But he took good care not to: he adopted the moral code of his stepfather without questioning it. The famous resolutions which he made about 1862 and wrote down under the heading of *Hygiene, Conduct, Morality* are painfully puerile:

'Epitome of wisdom.
'Dress, prayer, work.
'Work necessarily induces sound morals, sobriety and chastity, and as a result good health, wealth, sustained and progressive genius and charity. *Age quod agis.*'

The words sobriety, chastity and work occur again and again in his writings, but they have no positive content. They did not provide him with a line of conduct and they did not enable him to solve the great problems of his relations with other people and with himself. They were simply a system of rigid and strictly negative defenses. Sobriety meant not taking intoxicants; chastity—not going back to those young women who gave him too kindly a welcome and whose names are preserved in his notebook; work—not putting off until tomorrow what could be done today; charity—not being irritable or bitter and not being indifferent to other people. Besides, he recognized that he possessed 'a sense of duty,' that is to say, he regarded the moral life as a constraint, as a bit which hurt the restive mouth, never as an agonizing quest or a genuine *élan* from the heart:

Un ange furieux fond du ciel comme un aigle,
Du mécréant saisit à plein poing les cheveux
Et dit, le secouant: 'Tu connaîtras la règle!
(Car je suis ton bon Ange, entends-tu?) Je le veux.'

A few crabbed, torturing imperatives whose content was disarming in its poverty—such were the values and rules which served as a basis for the whole of his moral life. When, after being harried by his mother and Ancelle, he suddenly bridled, it was never in order to tell them to their faces that their bourgeois virtues were horrible and stupid; it was to flaunt his vices, to bellow that he was very wicked indeed and might have been even worse:

> 'Do you imagine then that if I wanted I couldn't ruin you and bring you down to misery in your old age? Don't you know that I am cunning enough and eloquent enough to do it? But I restrain myself . . .'[21]

It is impossible that he didn't feel that, in meeting them like this on their own ground and behaving like a sulky child who stamps and exaggerates his faults, he was providing them with hostages and aggravating his own case. But he was pig-headed. It was in the name of those values that he wanted absolution and he preferred to be condemned by them rather than to be whitewashed in the name of a wider and more fruitful ethic which he should have invented himself. His attitude during the trial was still stranger. Not once did he attempt to

[21] Letter of March 17th, 1862. (*Lettres inédites à sa mère,* Paris, 1918, p. 261. Not part of the Conard edition of the complete works.)

defend the content of his book; not once did he try to explain to the judges that he did not accept the moral code of 'cops' and pimps. On the contrary, he invoked it himself. That was the basis on which he was prepared to argue; and, rather than question whether their interdict was well founded, he accepted the secret shame of lying about the meaning of his work. Sometimes, indeed, he presented it simply as a distraction and he demanded in the name of Art for Art's sake the right to imitate passions from outside without experiencing them. At other times, he claimed that it was a work of edification which was intended to inspire a horror of vice. It was not until nine years later that he dared to admit the truth to Ancelle:

> 'Must I tell you—you who haven't guessed any more than the rest—that into this *atrocious* book I put the whole of my *heart*, the whole of my *tenderness*, the whole of my *religion* (travestied), the whole of my *hatred*? It's true that I shall say the opposite, that I shall swear by all the gods that it's a work of *pure art*, monkey tricks, *juggling*, and I shall be lying like a trooper. [22]

He allowed himself to be condemned; he accepted his judges. He even wrote a letter to the Empress saying that he 'had been treated by Justice with an admirable courtesy.' [23] Better still, he postulated a social rehabilitation: first a decoration, then the Academy. He took

[22] Letter of February 18th, 1866. (*Lettres*, 1841–1866, Mercure de France, 1906, p. 522.)
[23] *Corres. gén.*, 2, p. 100.

sides with his executioners, with Ancelle, Aupick and the Imperial police force against all those who like George Sand and Hugo wanted to set men free. He asked for the whip; he wanted them to make him practise the virtues which they preached:

'If, when a man developed habits of laziness, dreaminess and feebleness to the point of always putting off the important thing till the morrow, another man woke him up in the morning with hard lashes of a whip and whipped him mercilessly until, though unable to work for pleasure, he worked through fear, wouldn't this man—the man with the whip—be a true friend and benefactor?'

The least thing, a change of mind, a mere look into the eyes of these idols would have been enough to make his chains fall at once to the ground; he didn't do it. All his life he was content to judge his failings and let them be judged by accepted standards. It was he, the *poète maudit* of the banned poems, who sat down one day and wrote:

'It has been necessary at all times and in all countries to have gods and prophets to instil [virtue] into a brutalized humanity and . . . man *alone* would have been incapable of inventing it.' [24]

Can you imagine a more complete abdication? Baudelaire proclaims that he alone would have been incapable of discovering virtue, that there was not a germ of it in him, that left to himself he would not even have been

[24] *l'Art romantique*, p. 97.

49

able to understand its meaning. The principal characteristic of this virtue, which was revealed by the prophets and inculcated forcibly by the whips of priests and ministers, was to be beyond the power of individual men. They would have been incapable of inventing it and they were unable to doubt its validity: let them be content to receive it like a heavenly manna.

Baudelaire's Christian upbringing will certainly be blamed for this; and there is no doubt that it left a deep impress on him. But look at the distance travelled by another Christian—a Protestant, it is true—by André Gide. In the fundamental conflict between his sexual anomaly and accepted morality, he took sides with the former against the latter, and has gradually eaten away the rigorous principles which impeded him like an acid. In spite of a thousand relapses, he has moved forward towards *his* morality; he has done his utmost to invent a new Table of the Law. Yet the impress of Christianity on him was just as deep as it was on Baudelaire; but he wanted to free himself from other peoples' Good; he refused from the first to allow himself to be treated like a black sheep. In a similar situation he made a different choice; he wanted his conscience to be clear, and he understood that he could only achieve liberation by a radical and gratuitous invention of Good and Evil. Why did Baudelaire, the born creator, the poet of creation, suddenly balk at the last moment? Why did he waste his time and energy in preserving a norm which turned him into a guilty man? Why didn't he rise in wrath against this heteronomy which from the outset condemned his

50

conscience and his will to remain for ever a bad con-
science and a bad will?

Let us return to his famous 'difference.' The creative
act does not allow us to enjoy it. The man who creates
is transported, during the period of creation, beyond sin-
gularity into the pure sky of freedom. He *is* no longer
anything: he *makes*. No doubt he constructs an objective
individuality outside himself; but while he is working on
it, it is indistinguishable from himself. And later on he
no longer enters into that objective individuality; he re-
mains in front of it like Moses on the threshold of the
Promised Land. We shall see in due course that Baude-
laire wrote his poems in order to rediscover his own
image in them. That, however, could not satisfy him for
long. It was in his everyday life that he wanted to enjoy
his otherness. The great freedom which creates values
emerges in the void, and he was frightened of it. A sense
of contingency, unjustifiability and gratuitousness assails
the man who tries to bring a new reality into the world
and leaves him no respite. If it is in fact an absolutely new
reality, then it is something for which no one asked and
which no one expected to see on earth; and it remains
superfluous like its author.

Baudelaire asserted his singularity against the back-
ground of a stable world. He asserted it first of all against
his mother and his stepfather in a mood of rage and re-
volt. It was in fact a revolt and not a revolutionary act.
The revolutionary wants to change the world; he tran-
scends it and moves toward the future, towards an order
of values which he himself invents. The rebel is careful

to preserve the abuses from which he suffers so that he can go on rebelling against them. He always shows signs of a bad conscience and of something resembling a feeling of guilt. He does not want to destroy or transcend the existing order; he simply wants to rise up against it. The more he attacks it, the more he secretly respects it. In the depths of his heart he preserves the rights which he challenges in public. If they disappeared, his own *raison d'être* would disappear with them. He would suddenly find himself plunged into a gratuitousness which frightens him. It never occurred to Baudelaire to destroy the idea of the family. On the contrary, it could be argued that he never progressed beyond the stage of childhood.

The child takes his parents for gods. Their actions like their judgments are absolute. They are the incarnation of universal Reason, law, the meaning and purpose of the world. When the eye of these divine beings is turned on him, their look is enough to justify him at once to the very roots of his existence. It confers on him a definite, sacred character. Since they are infallible, it follows that they *see* him as he really *is*. There is no room in his mind for hesitation or doubt. True, all that he sees of himself is the vague succession of his moods, but the gods have made themselves the guardians of his eternal essence. He knows that it exists; even though he can have no direct experience of it, he realizes that his *truth* does not consist in what he can know of himself, but that it is hidden in the large, terrible yet gentle eyes which are turned towards him. He is a real essence among other real essences; he has *his* place in the world—an absolute place in an absolute world. Everything is complete; everything is just; everything that is, had to be. Baudelaire never ceased to regret the *verts paradis des amours enfantines*. He defined genius as 'childhood regained at will.' He believed that 'the child sees everything as a novelty; he is always intoxicated.' But he omitted to tell us that it is a very special form of intoxication. It is true that everything is novel for the child, but this novelty has already been seen, named and classified by other people. Every object comes to him with a label attached to it. It is eminently reassuring and sacred because the eye of grown-up people still hovers over it. Far from exploring unknown realms, the child turns over the pages of an album, counts the specimens in a herbal, does the owner's round. It was for the absolute security of childhood that Baudelaire yearned. The drama begins when the child grows up, becomes a head taller than his parents and looks over their shoulders. For behind them there is nothing; by overtaking his parents and perhaps by judging them he has the experience of his own transcendence. His father and mother have shrunk. Just look at them—thin and mediocre, unjustifiable and unjustified. The noble thoughts, which once reflected the universe, are reduced to the level of opinions and moods. He suddenly finds that the world has to be remade. All the places and even the order of things are disputed; and since he is no longer a thought in a divine Reason, since the look which fixed him is no more than a tiny light among other tiny lights, the child loses his essence and his truth. The vague moods and confused thoughts which once seemed to him the broken reflection of his metaphysical reality become his only mode of existence. At a stroke the duties, rites, the precise, limited obligations have vanished. Unjustified and unjustifiable, he suddenly becomes aware of his terrible freedom. Everything still has to begin. He suddenly emerges in solitude and the void.

It was this that Baudelaire wanted to avoid at any price. His parents remained hateful idols—but still idols. He assumed in their presence an attitude of resentment, but not of criticism. The *otherness* on which he insisted had nothing in common with the great metaphysical solitude which is the lot of each and all of us. The law of solitude might, indeed, be expressed in these terms: No man can place on others the burden of justifying his existence. It was precisely this that terrified Baudelaire. Solitude filled him with horror. He returned to the subject a hundred times in his letters to his mother. He described it as 'atrocious,' 'reducing him to despair.' Asselineau tells us that he could not bear to be alone for an hour. And it will be realized that it was not a question of physical isolation, but of the 'emergence in the void' which was the price of uniqueness. He insisted that he was *another person* certainly, but *another person among other people*. His disdainful otherness remained a social tie between himself and the people whom he despised. They had to be there in order to recognize his otherness, as we can see from a curious passage in *Fusées:*

'When I've inspired universal horror and disgust, I shall have overcome solitude.'

For to feel horror and disgust at Baudelaire was still a way not merely of paying attention, but of paying a great deal of attention to him. Think of it—horror! And if horror and disgust were universal, so much the better. It meant that everybody was taken up with him at every moment of the day. As he saw it, therefore, solitude possessed a social function. The pariah was banned by society, but precisely because in this way he became the object of a social act his solitude was consecrated and was even necessary to the proper functioning of institutions. Baudelaire seemed to expect his singularity to be consecrated and invested with a quasi-institutional character. Instead of depriving him of every place in the universe and of all rights to a place, like the human solitude of which he had had a glimpse and rejected, it actually gave him a place and conferred privileges and obligations on him. For this reason it was his parents whom he asked to recognize his place. His first aim, which was to punish them by making them understand the extent to which they were in the wrong, would be achieved when he had made them see the state of abandonment in which they had left him, the contemptuous uniqueness of which he was so proud but which also earned him the contempt of other people. It was in his parents that he must arouse horror; and the horror which gripped the gods when confronted by their creature would be at once their punishment and his consecration. People have taken every opportunity of attributing an unresolved Oedipus complex to him, but it matters little whether or not he desired his mother. I should rather say that he refused to resolve the theological complex which transforms parents into gods. He refused to resolve it because it was necessary in order to evade the law of solitude and find in other people a remedy against gratuitousness, to confer on other people, or rather on *certain* other people, a sacred character. What he wanted was neither friendship, love, nor relations on equal terms. He had no friends or at most a few intimates among the riff-raff. He wanted judges—beings whom he could deliberately place beyond the fundamental law of contingency, beings who existed simply because they had the right to exist and whose decrees conferred on him in his turn a stable and sacred 'nature.' He was ready to appear guilty in their eyes; and 'guilty in their eyes' meant absolutely guilty. But the guilty man has his function in the theocratic universe. He has his function and his rights. He has a right to censure, to punishment and to repentance. He co-operates with the universal order and his misdoing invests him with a religious dignity, a place apart in the hierarchy of beings. He is protected by a look which is indulgent or angry. Turn again to *la Géante:*

> *J'eusse aimé vivre auprès d'une jeune géante*
> *Comme aux pieds d'une reine un chat voluptueux.*

His dearest wish was to attract the attention of a giantess, to see himself through her eyes like a domestic animal, to lead the easy-going, sensual, perverse life of a cat in an aristocratic society where giants, where men-gods decided on the meaning of the universe and on the final end of his own life for him without even consulting him. He wanted to enjoy the limited independence of a *bête de luxe,* idle and useless, whose games were protected by the seriousness of its masters. In addition to this, we certainly find traces of masochism in his reverie. Baudelaire himself described it as Satanic because in it he explicitly

56

identified himself with an animal. And wasn't it necessarily masochistic to the extent to which his need of consecration led him to turn himself into an *object* for those large, serious beings? It will no doubt be argued that Baudelaire regretted the condition of the suckling, who is washed, fed and dressed by strong beautiful hands, even more than that of a cat. This is perfectly true, but it was not the result of some sort of technical hitch which is supposed to have arrested his development or of a traumatism which in any case cannot be proved. If he regretted his infancy, it was because in infancy he was free from the worry of living, because he enjoyed the complete luxury of being an object for tender adults who scolded him, but who were full of solicitude for him; because he could during infancy—and only during infancy—realize his dream of feeling that he was completely enveloped by a look.

But in order that there could be no appeal against the judgment which gave Baudelaire his place in the universe, it was essential that the motives which inspired him should be absolute. In other words, at the same time that he refused to challenge the sacred character of his judges, Baudelaire refused to question the idea of Good on which their decrees were founded. If his guilt was to be absolute, if his singularity was to be *metaphysical,* it followed that there must be an absolute Good. For Baudelaire this Good was not an object of love nor was it merely an abstract imperative; it was contained in a look—a look that ordered and condemned. The poet reversed the normal relations. For him it was not the law which preceded the judge, but the judge who pre-

ceded the law. Next, was the look—the look which trans-
fixed him, put him in his place and objectified him, the
great look which was 'the bearer of Good and Evil'—the
look of his mother, of General Aupick or of God 'who
sees all'? It was all the same. In *la Fanfarlo,* which ap-
peared in 1847, Baudelaire professed atheism. 'Just as he
had once been fanatically devout, he was now a fanatical
atheist.' He seems to have lost the faith after a pious and
mystical youth. In the years that followed, he does not
appear to have recovered his faith except during the crisis
of 1861; and during one of the very last years in which
he was still in full possession of his faculties, in 1864, he
wrote to Ancelle.

'I will explain with patience all my reasons for
feeling disgusted with the human race. When I am
absolutely alone, I shall seek a religion . . . and at
the moment of death I shall abjure this last religion
as a sign of my disgust at universal stupidity. You
can see that I haven't changed.' [25]

It would appear from this that Catholic critics are de-
cidedly bold in claiming that he was one of them. But
whether he was a believer or not matters little. Even if
he did not regard the existence of God as a reality, it was
nevertheless one of the poles of his imaginary reveries.
He wrote in *Fusées:*

'Even if God did not exist, Religion would still be
holy and *Divine.*

[25] *Lettres,* 1841–66, p. 386

'God is the only being who in order to reign does not even need to exist.'

What counted therefore even more than the mere existence of this all-powerful being was his nature and functions. Now it must be noticed that Baudelaire's God was a God of terror. He sent his angels to torment sinners. His law was the Old Testament. There was no intercessor between him and mankind. Christ seems to have been unknown to Baudelaire and Jean Massin himself speaks of 'his tragic ignorance of the Saviour.' [26] It was because it was not so much a question of being saved as judged, or rather it was because salvation lay in the judgment itself which put everyone in his proper place in an ordered world. When Baudelaire lamented the fact that he did not possess the faith, it was always the witness and the judge whose absence he regretted:

'I desire with all my heart . . . to believe that an *external* invisible being is interested in my fate. But what does one do to believe it?' [27]

What he missed was neither divine love nor grace, but the pure 'external' look which would take him up and envelop him. He adopted the same point of view in *Mon coeur mis à nu* when he puts forward that strange proof of the divine existence:

[26] *Baudelaire devant la douleur* (Collection 'Hier et Demain'), No. 10, Paris, 1944, p. 19.
[27] Letter to his mother of March 6th, 1861. (*Lettres inédites à sa mère*, p. 224.)

'*Calculation in favor of God.* Nothing exists without a purpose. Therefore my existence has a purpose. What purpose? I do not know. It is, therefore, not I who have determined this purpose. Therefore it is someone who is wiser than I. I must therefore pray to that person to enlighten me. It is the wisest course.'

In these passages we meet again his obstinate belief in a pre-established order of ends, and Baudelaire reveals once more his desire to be incorporated into a hierarchy by the look of a Creator. But this God without charity, this God of justice who punishes and whose whip is blessed, who neither gives nor demands love is indistinguishable from General Aupick, that other father with a whip who filled his son with such abominable fear. It has been seriously maintained that Baudelaire was in love with General Aupick. Such idiocy is not even worth refuting, but what remains true is that he demanded that severity of which he complained throughout his life. And the part played by the General was of capital importance in the process of self-punishment which will be discussed later on. It is also true that the terrible Aupick seems after his death to have become incarnate in the poet's mother. But at this point the case becomes extremely complex. Mme. Aupick was certainly the only person for whom Baudelaire ever felt affection. In his eyes she remained linked with a free and gentle childhood. From time to time he reminded her sadly:

'During my childhood there was a period when I loved you passionately. Listen and don't be afraid to read on. I have never said so much about it to you before. I remember a drive in a fly. You had just come out of a nursing home where you'd been sent and to prove that you'd been thinking about your son you showed me some pen-and-ink drawings which you'd done for me. You think I've got a terrible memory, don't you? I remember later on the Place Saint-André-des-Arts and Neuilly. Long outings and constant affection! I remember the *quais* which were so sad in the evening. Ah! for me those were the happy days of motherly love . . . I was always living in you; you belonged to me alone. You were at once an idol and a friend.' [28]

He certainly loved her as a woman even more than as a mother. While the General was still alive, he liked arranging adulterous meetings with her in museums. And during the last years of his life he still wrote to her in a tone of light and charming gallantry:

'[At Honfleur] I shall be, not happy—that's impossible—but tranquil enough to spend the whole of my days working and the whole of my evenings amusing you and paying my court to you.' [29]

Yet he had no illusions about her. She was frail and obstinate, capricious and 'fantastic'; she had no taste; her character was at once 'absurd and generous'; she trusted the first comer blindly rather than her son. But little by little Aupick contaminated her. His severity left its mark

[28] Letter of May 6th, 1861. (*Lettres inédites à sa mère*, p. 227.)
[29] Letter of March 26th, 1860 (*ibid.*, p. 195).

on her and after her husband's death she assumed in spite of herself his crushing role of judge. For Baudelaire simply had to have a witness. She possessed neither the strength nor the inclination to punish him, yet he trembled in front of this insignificant little woman whom he knew through and through. He admitted it to her in 1860 when he was nearly forty years old:

'I must tell you one thing which you've probably never guessed—I'm very, very frightened of you.' [30]

He daren't write to her 'when he was not pleased with himself.' And for whole days together he used to carry her letters about with him in his pocket without daring to open them:

'Sometimes because I'm afraid of your scoldings and sometimes because I'm frightened of distressing news about your health, I daren't open your letters. When I see a letter in front of me I'm not brave . . .' [31]

He knew that her reproaches were unjust, blind, unintelligent, that they were due to the influence of Ancelle or one of her neighbors at Honfleur or a priest whom he detested. No matter. For him they were verdicts against which there was no appeal. He had invested her in spite of herself with the supreme power of judging him; and even if he challenged one by one the grounds of her judgment the verdict remained unshaken. He chose to put himself in the position of the guilty person. His

[30] *ibid.*, p. 195.   [31] *ibid.*, loc. cit.

letters are confessions in the Russian style. Since he knew that she blamed him, he used his wits to provide her with reasons; he 'piled things on.' But above all else he was anxious to redeem himself in his mother's eyes. One of his most burning, his most constant hopes was that the day would come when she would solemnly reverse her judgment of him. At the age of forty-one when he was going through his religious crisis, he prayed to God to give him 'the necessary strength to carry out all [his] duties and to grant [his] mother a long enough life to enjoy [his] transformation.' This wish recurs often in his correspondence. We feel that it was of capital, of metaphysical importance for him. The final judgment for which he was waiting was a *consecration* of his life. If his mother were to die before the ceremony took place, Baudelaire's life would be ruined; it would go on in a completely haphazard manner, would suddenly be invaded by the appalling gratuitousness which he rejected with all his strength. But if on the contrary the day came when she declared that she was satisfied, she would have set her seal on his tormented existence. Baudelaire would achieve salvation because his big vague conscience would be ratified.

But this severity, which at times was so distilled that it was no more than the pure look of God and at other times was incarnate in a general or an ageing futile woman, could also assume other forms. Sometimes it was Napoleon III's magistrates and sometimes members of the French Academy who were invested with an unexpected dignity. It has been claimed that the condemnation of the *Fleurs du mal* came as a surprise to Baudelaire. That is untrue. He expected it as we can see from his letters to Poulet-Malassis. We might even go so far as to say that he sought condemnation. And, in the same way, when he decided to stand for the Academy, he wanted judges rather than voters because he felt that the vote of the Immortals would be his rehabilitation. As François Porché has well said: 'Baudelaire therefore came to think that if he were admitted to the Academy, the suspicion which surrounded him would vanish on the spot. No doubt, but this argument contains a vicious circle because it was this very suspicion which prevented the poet from having the slightest chance of success.' [32] Baudelaire was irritated by the continual chatter of Ancelle whose guilelessness prevented him from taking his place on the judges' bench, so by a sudden impulse he took another adviser, a certain M. Jaquotot. He announced that he was delighted with him:

'With his languishing airs and his love of pleasure, he seems to me to be a wise man. At any rate, he has a sense of propriety as he proved in the searching but friendly cross-examination to which he subjected me.' [33]

Now this is the way in which M. Jaquotot expressed himself about Baudelaire in a letter to Mme. Aupick:

'He calmed down a good deal and I made him see how unbecoming such behavior was towards a re-

[32] *La Vie douloureuse de Charles Baudelaire* ('Le Roman des Grandes Existences,' No. 6), Paris, 1926, p. 244.
[33] *Corres. gén.*, 2, p. 146.

spected friend and a friend of his mother's. While admitting his faults, he persisted in his refusal to have anything to do with him. . . . I believe that he was speaking the truth because it is very much in his own interests to behave well and not to mislead you or me either.'[34]

We are therefore forced to conclude that Baudelaire liked this discreetly protective line. Moreover, he himself explained to his mother, with a sort of fatuity, that he had been scolded:

'M. Jaquotot,' he writes, 'began by reproaching me sharply for my violence.'

And he adds:

'M. Jaquotot asked whether I would submit to some sort of supervision by him if he took Ancelle's place. I told him that I should be perfectly agreeable.'[35]

There he is, then, overcome with delight at changing masters. So true is it that each of us fashions his destiny in his own image that Baudelaire, who from the first elected to live under guardianship, found his cup filled to overflowing. The existence of the family council was no doubt the source of innumerable humiliations and embarrassments for him, and he sincerely detested it; but for such a connoisseur of whips and judges this particular tribunal was indispensable; it satisfied a need. It would

[34] *ibid.*, p. 166. [35] *ibid.*, pp. 163–4.

be a mistake therefore to regard it as an unfortunate accident which wrecked his career. It was a very precise image of the poet's aspirations and, as it were, an organ which was necessary to preserve his equilibrium. Thanks to the tribunal, he was always tied to his duties, always in chains. All his life these imposing grave-faced men, whom Kafka would have called 'Gentlemen,' had the right to speak to him in a tone of fatherly severity; he had to beg for money like a spendthrift student and he never received any except through the kindliness of these numerous 'fathers' whom the law had given him. He was an eternal minor, a middle-aged adolescent who lived in a constant state of rage and hatred, but under the vigilant and reassuring protection of others.

And as though it were not enough to have all these guardians and trustees, all these portly gentlemen who decided his fate between them, he chose a secret guardian who was the strictest of them all—Joseph de Maistre, the final incarnation of the *Other*. 'It was he,' said Baudelaire, 'who taught me to think.' In order to feel completely at his ease, ought he not to occupy a specially designated place in the natural and social hierarchy? The austere thinker who was in bad faith taught him the intoxicating arguments of conservatism. For everything holds together. In a society in which he wanted to be the *enfant terrible,* there had to be an *élite* of people armed with whips:

'In politics, the true saint is the man who uses his whip and kills the people for their own good.'

That, no doubt, was written with a shiver of pleasure. For if politics killed the people in the name of the Good of the people, then this Good was all the more surely out of reach. What security, since the victim was forbidden to decide on it and since in the throes of his sufferings he was told that it was for *his* Good—the Good which was unknown to him—that he was dying! It was also necessary that this very strict hierarchy should be pre-established and that the men with whips should make themselves its guardians. Lastly, privileges and anathemas must not be the result of merits which were acquired voluntarily or of deliberate wrongdoing. On the contrary, they had to overtake the victims *a priori* like a malediction. That is why Baudelaire declared that he was anti-Semitic. The machine was ready and Baudelaire in the place reserved for him. He was not to be one of the flagellators—for above them there was nothing except the void and gratuitousness—but with the utmost relish he would be the first of the whipped.

But we must not forget that it was by knowingly doing Evil and by what he called his 'conscience in Evil' that Baudelaire gave his adherence to Good. If we discount his moments of fervor, which in any case were purely transitory and ineffectual, it seems that for Baudelaire the moral law was only there in order to be transgressed. It was not enough to ask proudly for the fate of the pariah; he had to commit sins at every moment of the day. At this point our account is complicated by the intervention of a fresh dimension—the dimension of freedom.

For Baudelaire's attitude towards his own singularity was by no means simple. In a sense he wanted to enjoy it in the same way that the Others did which meant standing in front of his freedom as though it were an object. He wanted his inner eye to bring it into being in the same way that the whiteness of the white blackbird comes into being under the eyes of the other blackbirds. It had to be there, settled, stable, tranquil in the manner of an essence. But on the other hand, his pride could never be satisfied by a form of originality which had been passively accepted and of which he himself was not the author. He wanted to feel that he had made himself the person he was; and, as we have seen, from childhood he passionately assumed his 'separation' because he was afraid of having it thrust upon him. No doubt his failure to discover in himself what it was that made him irreplaceable drove him to appeal to others and to ask them to turn him into a different person by their judgment of him; but he could never admit that he was the pure *object* of their gaze. In the same way that he wanted to *objectify* the vague flux of his inner life, he tried to interiorize the *thing* that he was for other people by transforming it into a plan of himself which had been freely adopted. At bottom it was always a question of the same continual effort towards recovery. When applied to the inner life, recovery meant treating consciousness as a thing so that he would be in a better position to take possession of it. But when it was a question of the being you were for other people, you could recover by assimilating *the thing* to a free consciousness. This paradoxical alternation came from the ambiguity of the idea of *pos-*

session. A man can only possess himself if he creates himself; but if he creates himself he escapes from himself. There is only one *thing* that a man can ever possess; but if he is a thing in this world, he loses that creative freedom which is the foundation of appropriation. And then Baudelaire, who possessed a sense of freedom and a taste for it, became afraid of it when he descended into the limbo of his consciousness. He saw that freedom led necessarily to absolute solitude and to a total responsibility. He wanted to run away from the anguish of the isolated individual who knows that he must accept total responsibility without recourse to the world or to Good and Evil. No doubt he did want to be free, but free within the framework of a ready-made universe. Just as he planned the conquest of a solitude which would have people in it and would be consecrated, so he tried to win a freedom which only carried a limited responsibility. No doubt he did want to create himself, but he wanted to create himself in the image which other people had of him. He wanted to be a something whose very nature was a contradiction—he wanted to be a *freedom-thing*. He fled from the terrifying truth that freedom is only limited by itself and he tried to force it into an external framework. He merely asked that it should be just sufficient for him to be able to claim as his own handiwork the image other people had of him. His ideal was to be his own cause, which would have soothed his pride, and nevertheless to have produced himself in conformity with a divine plan, which would have calmed his anguish and justified his existence. In short, he asked to be free which was tantamount to saying that he was gratuitous and unjustifiable in his very independence—and to be *consecrated*—which implied that society had imposed his particular function and even his own nature on him.

It is not open to anyone who chooses to assert his freedom in the world of Joseph de Maistre. The paths are marked out, the aims fixed, the orders given. There is only one way for the upright man—conformity. Now that was just what Baudelaire wanted. Did not theocracy limit human freedom to the choice of the means which must be used to attain ends which were beyond discussion?

On the other hand, Baudelaire despised *usefulness* and action. Now it is precisely any act which uses means in order to achieve a given end which deserves the name of useful. But Baudelaire had too much sense of creation to accept the humble role of workman. At this point we can begin to understand the significance of his vocation as a poet. His poems are like substitutes for the creation of Good which he had renounced. They reveal the gratuitousness of conscience; they are completely useless; and they assert in every line the existence of what he called supernaturalism. At the same time, they remain in the sphere of the imaginary, leaving untouched the question of primary and absolute creation. They are substitutes because each represents a symbolical satisfaction of a desire for complete autonomy, of a demiurgic thirst for creation. Yet Baudelaire could not be entirely satisfied by a form of activity which was derivative and, so to speak, underhand. He therefore found himself in a contradictory position. He wanted to display his freewill by working only for his own ends; but on the other hand, he wanted to hide his gratuitousness and limit his responsibility by accepting the pre-established ends of theocracy. It must be clearly understood that it was not a question of picking forbidden fruits *although* they were forbidden, but of picking them *because* they were forbidden. When a man chooses of his own accord to commit a crime in his own interest, he may be harmful or horrible; but he is not doing Evil for Evil's sake because he does not in the least disapprove of what he is doing. Only other people who see him from outside are in a position to decide that he is wicked; but if we could look into his conscience, we should only see an interplay of motives which might perhaps be crude, but which would certainly be in harmony with one another. To do Evil for Evil's sake means that you do exactly the opposite of what you continue to recognize as Good. It means that you wish what you don't want—because you continue to abhor the powers of wickedness—and do not wish what you do want—because Good must always be defined as the end and object of your deepest will. That was precisely Baudelaire's attitude. There was the same difference between his actions and those of a common criminal as between the celebrant of a Black Mass and an atheist. The atheist doesn't bother about God because he had made up his mind once for all that God doesn't exist. But the priest who celebrates a Black Mass hates God because He is kind and flouts Him because He is respectable. He applies his will to the negation of the established order, but at the same time he preserves this order and asserts his belief in its existence more strongly than ever. If he ceased to do so for a single moment, the internal harmony of his conscience would be restored and Evil would be transformed on the spot into Good, with the result that he would transcend all orders which did not emanate from himself and would emerge in the void without God, without excuses and saddled with a total responsibility. Now the anguish which defines 'conscience in Evil,' is clearly expressed in the passage we quoted above on the double postulation: 'There are in every man at every hour of the day two simultaneous postulations, one towards God, the other towards Satan.' It must be understood that in actual fact these two postulations are not independent, are not two autonomous and opposing forces which are applied simultaneously at the same point, but that one is a function of the other. For freedom to cause giddiness it must choose in the theocratic world to be infinitely in the wrong. In this way it becomes *unique* in a world entirely directed towards Good; but it must adhere completely to Good, must preserve and reinforce it in order to retain the power of plunging into Evil. And the man who is damned enters into a solitude which is like a feeble image of the great solitude of the man who is really free. He is in fact just as lonely as he wants to be and not a whit more. The world remains ordered; ends remain absolute and intangible; the hierarchy is not disrupted. If he repents and ceases to desire Evil he will suddenly find that his dignity has been restored. In a sense he does create. In a universe in which every element is sacrificed as a contribution to the grandeur of the whole, it is he who is the cause of singularity, that is to say, the rebellion of a fragment; of a detail. It follows from this that something has come into being which did not exist before, which nothing can efface and which was in no way prepared by the rigorous economy of the world. It is a work of luxury which is gratuitous and unpredictable. Let us be clear about the relations between evil and poetry. When on top of everything else poetry takes evil for its subject, the two forms of creation which are based on limited responsibility are brought together and merge into one another, and we suddenly get a *fleur du mal*. But the deliberate creation of Evil, in the sense of wrong, is an acceptance and recognition of Good. It pays tribute to Good and by describing itself as wicked admits that it is relative and derivative, that without Good it would not exist. It therefore contributes in a roundabout way to the glorification of the rule. Better still, it proclaims that it is the void. Since everything which is serves Good, Evil does not exist. As Claudel observes: the worst is not always certain. And the guilty person has the feeling that his wrongdoing is at once a challenge to being itself and a prank which glides over being without harming it and is of no consequence. The sinner is an *enfant terrible,* but at bottom he is good and knows it. He regards himself as the prodigal son whose father will never cease to await his return. By refusing the useful and devoting all his efforts and care to cultivating anomalies which are completely ineffectual and without any real existence, he resigns himself to being taken for an adolescent playing a game. It is this, indeed, which gives him such a sense of perfect security in the midst of his terrors. He plays and is left alone. In short, his very freedom—his freedom to do evil—is a concession. There is no doubt about damnation; but the sinner suffers so much, retains such an acute feeling for Good while actually committing his sins, that he never really doubts his ultimate forgiveness. Hell is all very well for the crude, smug sins, but the soul of a man who desires Evil for Evil's sake is an exquisite blossom. It would be just as much out of place among the vulgar mob of sinners as a duchess surrounded by 'tarts' at Saint-Lazare. Besides, Baudelaire who belonged to this aristocracy of Evil did not believe sufficiently deeply in God to be really afraid of Hell. For his damnation was of this world and it was never final. Damnation meant blame from Other People, General Aupick's look, his mother's unopened letters in his pocket, the family council and Ancelle's reassuring chatter. But a day would surely come when his debts would be paid off, when his mother would give him absolution. He never doubted his final redemption. It is easy to see why for the time being he wanted severe judges: indulgence, tolerance and understanding would weaken his freedom by making him feel less guilty. So he became perverse. Jules Lemaître said quite rightly: 'Since nothing is comparable to the depth and profundity of religious feelings (on account of the love and terror they contain) we come back to them and revive them in ourselves, and we do so at the same time that we go in search of sensations which are most directly condemned by the beliefs from which our feelings are derived. In this way we arrive at something marvellously artificial. . . .'[36]

There is of course no doubt that Baudelaire enjoyed

[36] *Journal des Débats,* 1887.

his sins, but we still have to explain the nature of his enjoyment. When Lemaître adds that Baudelaire's attitude does indeed represent 'the supreme effort of intellectual and emotional Epicureanism,' he misses the point completely. It was not a question for Baudelaire of deliberately titillating his pleasures. On the contrary, he might very well have replied in all good faith that he poisoned his pleasures. And nothing could have been farther from his thoughts than the very idea of an Epicurean pursuit of pleasure. But when sin led to pleasure (*volupté*), pleasure profited from the sin. *Volupté* seems at first to have been singled out from all the other sins. Since it was forbidden, it was useless and a luxury. What was more, since it was sought out against the established order by a freedom which incurred damnation in order to bring it into being, it appeared to be analogous to creation. Crude pleasures, the simple satisfaction of appetites, rivet us to nature at the same time that they make us banal. Now Baudelaire's *volupté* was an exquisite rarity. It was because in the moment that followed it the sinner would be overwhelmed by remorse that it appeared to be the unique, the privileged moment of the commitment. It was through *volupté* that he became guilty and while he was in the act of succumbing, the eyes of his judges never left him. He sinned *in public* and while he was aware of the horrible security of being changed into an object by the moral condemnation which his action incurred, he felt the pride of being free and creative. This turning on himself, which necessarily accompanied the sin, prevented him from really submerging himself in his pleasures. He never became so

75

involved that he lost his senses. On the contrary, it was in the moment of the bitterest sensual pleasure that he really found himself. He was truly himself in such conditions, free and condemned, creator and criminal. And this self-enjoyment placed, as it were, the distance necessary for their contemplation between him and his pleasures. Baudelaire's *volupté* was restrained, was more scrutinized than felt. You didn't plunge into it; you brushed against it; it was as much a pretext as an end; freedom and remorse spiritualized it; it was refined by Evil and turned into something insubstantial:

'As for myself, I say: the supreme and unique pleasure (*volupté*) of love lies in the certainty that one is doing *evil*.—And man and woman know from birth that the whole of pleasure is to be found in evil.'

And we understand now, but only now, this saying of Baudelaire's:

'When I was only a child I felt in my heart two contradictory sentiments, the horror of life and the ecstasy of life.'

Here again we must not regard the horror and the ecstasy as though they were independent of one another. His horror of life was a horror of the natural, a horror of the spontaneous exuberance of nature, a horror, too, of the soft living limbo of consciousness. It was also an adherence to the withered conservatism of Joseph de Maistre with its taste for controls and artificial categories. But the ecstasy of life came later and was carefully

76

shielded by all these barriers. It was a very Baudelairean mixture of contemplation and enjoyment, the spiritualized pleasure that he called *volupté,* the prudent dabbling in Evil when the whole body hung back and caressed without embracing. It has been said that he was impotent, and there is no doubt that he was not particularly attracted by physical possession which was too close to natural pleasure. He said contemptuously of woman that she is 'on heat and wants to be poked.' He realized that with intellectuals like himself 'the more [they] cultivate the arts, the less they copulate,' which might be taken for a personal admission. But life is not the same as nature. He admits in *Mon coeur mis à nu* that he had 'a very lively taste for life and pleasure.' That meant a carefully distilled life which was kept at a distance and recreated by freedom, and pleasure spiritualized by Evil. To put the matter in plain terms, he was more sensual than passionate. The temperamental man forgets himself in the intoxication of the senses; Baudelaire never forgot himself. He had a horror of the sexual act in the proper sense because it is natural and brutal and because at bottom it is a form of communication with the Other Person. *'Foutre* is the desire to enter into another and the artist never goes outside himself.' But there exist pleasures which can be enjoyed at a distance like seeing, fingering and smelling women's flesh. There is no doubt at all that these were the forms of pleasure in which he indulged. He was a *voyeur* and a fetichist precisely because such vices alleviated *volupté,* because they stood for possession at a distance and, so to speak, in a symbolical form. The *voyeur* never gives himself. An ob-

77

scene and discreet shiver passes through his whole person when, fully clothed, he contemplates a naked body without touching it. Baudelaire was doing wrong and he knew it; he possessed the other person at a distance and held himself back. After that, it matters little whether he sought satisfaction in solitary pleasures as some people have suggested or in what he called, with intentional brutality, *la fouterie*. Even in coitus he would have remained a solitary, an onanist, because at bottom all he enjoyed was his own sin. The essential thing is that he worshipped 'life,' but a life in chains, restrained, fingered, and that this impure love like a flower of evil came to birth on the humus of horror. It was for this reason that on the whole he thought of sin in the form of eroticism. The thousand other forms of evil—treachery, baseness, envy, brutality, avarice and many others besides—remained completely alien to him. He chose a sumptuous, aristocratic sin. He never joked at all about his real failings—laziness and 'procrastination.' He hated them and was dismayed by them because they were directed against his freedom and not against pre-established ends. In the same way the masochist will kiss the feet of a prostitute who slaps him in return for money and will perhaps kill the man who goes for him seriously. It was a question of a game of no consequence—a game with life, a game with Evil. But it was precisely because it was an empty game that Baudelaire enjoyed it. Nothing gave him a greater sensation of freedom and solitude than empty, sterile acts which produced nothing, a phantom evil which was pursued and suggested rather than realized. At the same time, the rights of Good were safeguarded; there had only been shivers of pleasure; he had slipped but without really compromising himself. We are told that Buffon wrote with his cuffs on; in the same way Baudelaire put on gloves for love-making.

From the double postulation onwards it becomes easy enough to describe Baudelaire's inner life. Through pride and rancor he tried all his life to *turn himself into a thing* in the eyes of other people and in his own. He wanted to take up his stand at a distance from the great social fête like a statue, like something definitive and opaque which could not be assimilated. In a word, we can say that he wanted to *be*—and by that we mean the obstinate, carefully defined mode of being which belongs to an object. But Baudelaire would never for a moment have tolerated in this being, which he wanted to force on the attention of others and enjoy himself, the passiveness and unconsciousness of a utensil. He certainly wanted to be an object, but not a thing which had come into being by mere chance. This thing was to be his very own; it would achieve salvation if it could be established that it had created itself and that it alone maintained its own being. This takes us back to the mode of the presence of consciousness and freedom which we will call *existence*. Baudelaire neither could nor would follow *being* or *existence* to the limit. He scarcely allowed himself to make a move towards one of them without at once seeking refuge in the other. If he felt that he was an object—and a guilty object—in the eyes of his chosen judges, he at once proceeded to assert his freedom against them either by the trumpetings of vice or by a remorse whose wing lifted him far above his own

79

nature or by a thousand other tricks which will become apparent later on. But if this carried him into the realm of freedom, he was seized with panic in face of his gratuitousness and the limits of his consciousness. He clung to a ready-made universe where Good and Evil were settled in advance and in which he occupied his appointed place. He chose to have a conscience which was always tormented, was always a bad conscience. His insistence on man's perpetual dualism, on the double postulation, on body and soul, on the horror and ecstasy of life, reflected his divided spirit. Because he wanted at the same time to be and to exist, because he continually fled from existence to being and from being to existence, he was nothing but a gaping wound. All his actions and each of his thoughts had two meanings—were dominated by two contradictory intentions which issued commands to one another and destroyed one another. He preserved Good in order to be able to do Evil, and if he did Evil it was in order to pay tribute to Good. If he departed from the Norm, it was in order to bring home to himself the power of Law, so that a look could judge him and classify him in spite of himself in the universal hierarchy; but if he recognized this Order and this supreme power explicitly, it was in order to escape from them and to become conscious of his solitude in sin. In these monsters which he worshipped he found first and foremost the indefeasible laws of the World in the sense that 'the exception proves the rule'; but he found them parodied and derided. Nothing about him was simple; he ended by losing himself in them and by writing in a state of despair: 'I have such a strange soul that I don't even recognize myself in it.' This strange soul lived in bad faith. There was indeed something in it which it hid from itself by perpetual flight. It chose not to choose *its* Good. Its profound sense of freedom, fighting shy of itself, borrowed from outside ready-made principles precisely because they were ready-made. We must not imagine like Lemaître that these complications were clearly and consciously willed and that Baudelaire made exclusive use of an Epicurean technique. In that case all his tricks would have been vain; he would have known himself too well to be taken in by them. The choice that he made of himself was much more deeply rooted in him. He was not aware of it because it was inseparable from himself. On the other hand, we must not equate a free choice of this kind with the obscure chemical changes which the psycho-analysts relegate to the unconscious. Baudelaire's choice was *his* consciousness, *his* essential plan. In a sense therefore he was so involved in it that it resembled a transparent image of himself. It was the light of his eye and the atmosphere of his thoughts; but there entered into this choice the determination not to give himself away, to embrace the whole of knowledge but not to make himself known. In short, his initial choice was initially made in bad faith. Baudelaire never believed completely in anything he thought or felt, in any of his sufferings or in any of his gritty *voluptés*. That was, perhaps, the real source of his sufferings. Let us be under no misapprehension about it—not to believe completely is not the same as to deny; bad faith is still faith. It should rather be said that Baudelaire's feelings had a sort of interior emptiness. He tried by a perpetual frenzy,

81

by an extraordinary nervousness to make up for their insufficiency. In vain. They sounded hollow. He reminds us of the neurasthenic who was convinced that he had an ulcerated stomach and who rolled shrieking and trembling on the floor, drenched in perspiration; but there was no pain. If we could put out of our minds the exaggerated vocabulary which Baudelaire used to describe himself, forget words like 'frightful,' 'nightmare' and 'horror' which occur on every page of the *Fleurs du mal,* and penetrate right into his heart we should perhaps find beneath the anguish, the remorse and the vibrating nerves something gentler and much more intolerable than the most painful of ills—Indifference. Not a languid indifference which had been provoked by some physiological inadequacy, but rather that fundamental impossibility of taking oneself completely seriously which usually goes with bad faith. All the characteristics which belong to the image that we have of him must therefore be seen as though they rested on a subtle and secret void. And we must not be taken in by the words which we use to describe him because they evoke and suggest something much more than he was. If we want to catch a glimpse of the lunar landscape of this distressed soul, let us remember that man is never anything but an imposture.

Since he chose Evil, it follows that he chose to feel guilty. It was through remorse that he realized his uniqueness and his freedom as a sinner. Throughout the whole of his life his feeling of guilt never left him. It was not a question of the tiresome consequences of his choice. With Baudelaire the importance of remorse was functional. It was remorse which made an act into a sinful act; a crime of which one does not repent is no longer a crime, but at most a piece of bad luck. It even seems that with Baudelaire remorse preceded the sin. Already at eighteen we find him saying in a letter to his mother that he has 'not dared to show himself to M. Aupick in all his ugliness.' He accuses himself of 'a multitude of failings which are no longer agreeable failings.' And while complaining rather slyly about the Lasègues, where he has been sent to lodge, he adds:

> 'It's perhaps a good thing to have been denuded and stripped of one's poetry. I understand better now what I lacked.' [37]

From that time onwards his self-accusations never ceased. And of course he was sincere, or rather his bad faith went so deep that he was no longer master of it. He had such a violent horror of himself that we can regard his life as a long series of self-inflicted punishments. Through self-punishment he redeemed himself and, according to an expression of which he was fond, 'rejuvenated' himself. But at the same time he set himself up as a guilty man. He disarmed his own wrong-doing, yet contrived to consecrate it for eternity. He identified his own judgment of himself with that of other people. It was as though he took a snapshot of his sinful freedom and fixed it for eternity. For eternity he *was* the most irreplaceable of sinners; but at that very moment he transcended it in the direction of a new freedom; fled from it towards Good as he fled from

[37] Letter of July 16th, 1839. (*Corres. gén.,* I, p. 8.)

Good towards Evil. And no doubt the punishment went beyond the present sin and by a much deeper and much more obscure impulse was aimed at that Bad Faith which was his besetting sin, which he would not admit and which he nevertheless tried to expiate. But he tried in vain to break out of the vicious circle in which he had trapped himself; the punishment was a favor like the crime: it was aimed at a wrong which was freely recognized as such by reference to ready-made standards. The first and the most constant of these self-inflicted punishments was undoubtedly his lucidity. We have seen the origins of this lucidity. From the first he took up his position on the plane of reflection because he *wanted* to grasp his otherness; but he came to use it as a whip. This 'conscience in evil' of which he boasted might sometimes be delicious, but he cultivated it primarily because it lacerated him like repentance. We have also seen that he identified this self-scrutiny with the scrutiny of the Other. He saw or tried to see himself as though he were another person; and it is certainly impossible really to see ourselves through other peoples' eyes because we are too close to ourselves. But if we don judge's robes, if our reflective consciousness apes disgust and indignation over the reflected consciousness, if, in order to qualify the reflected consciousness, it borrows its ideas and standards from an acquired system of morality, we may for a moment create the illusion that we have placed a *distance* between the act of reflection and the thing reflected. By means of a lucidity which was a method of punishment, Baudelaire endeavored to transform himself into an object in his own eyes. He explains that in addition, his merciless lucidity might, by a clever trick, assume the appearance of redemption:

'A ridiculous, cowardly or mean action, whose recollection upset me for a moment, is in complete contradiction with my real nature; my present nature, the very energy with which I contemplate it, the inquisitorial care with which I analyze and judge it are a proof of my lofty and divine aptitude for virtue. How many other people could one find in the world of men who are as skilful in judging themselves and as severe in self-condemnation as I?'[38]

It is true that he is speaking here of the opium-smoker, but hasn't he told us that a poisonous intoxication does not produce any important modifications in the personality of the intoxicated person? He is the smoker who condemns and absolves himself. This complex 'mechanism' is very Baudelairean. The moment I turn myself into an object, I also become a judge on account of the severity, from a social point of view, with which I treat myself; and freedom flies from the thing judged and takes up its abode in the judge. Thus by a fresh combination Baudelaire tried once again to unite existence and being. He was himself that severe freedom which always managed to escape condemnation because freedom itself was nothing but a condemnation. He was also the being who remained motionless in the act of wrongdoing while people watched and judged him. He was at once inside

[38] *Paradis artificiels.*

and outside, object and witness for himself; he introduced other peoples' eyes into himself so that he could look at himself as though he were another person; and the moment that he did see himself, his freedom asserted itself and escaped from everyone's sight because it was no longer anything but a look. There were, however, other forms of punishment. We might even say that Baudelaire's whole life was a punishment. I cannot discover in it an accident or any of those misfortunes which can be described as undeserved or unexpected. Everything seems to reflect his image; every happening appears to be a punishment which had been long meditated. He sought and found his family council, sought and found the condemnation of his poems, his rebuff by the Academy and that irritating form of celebrity which was so far removed from the fame of which he dreamed. He set out to make himself odious, to repel people and drive them away. He circulated rumors about himself of a kind which were calculated to humiliate him, in particular he left no stone unturned to make people believe that he was a pederast. 'Baudelaire,' said Buisson, 'was taken on board a merchant ship bound for India as an apprentice. He spoke with horror of the treatment which he received; and when we recall what this elegant young man must have been like, frail, almost a woman, and the sort of morals which prevailed among seamen, it is more than probable that he was telling the truth. We shuddered as we listened to him.'

On January 3rd, 1865, he wrote to Mme. Meurice from Brussels:

'I have been taken for a policeman (Serves me right!), for a pederast. (It was I who spread the story and *people believed me!*)' [39]

He was probably the source of the unfounded perfidious rumors reported by Charles Cousin that he had been expelled from the Lycée Louis-le-Grand for homosexuality. But he not only attributed vices to himself; he went so far as to make himself look ridiculous.

'Anyone else,' said Asselineau, 'would have died of the ridicule which he deliberately brought on himself for his own amusement and whose effects delighted him.'

The accounts of him by people who knew him have an indefinable tone of good-natured protectiveness which seems intolerable to the contemporary reader and which was certainly the result of his eccentricities. He himself wrote in *Fusées:*

'When I've aroused universal horror and disgust, I shall have conquered solitude.'

And certainly there is more than one explanation of this desire to disgust other people just as there is more than one explanation of all Baudelaire's attitudes. But there is no doubt that we must consider it in the first place as a tendency to self-punishment. There was nothing down to his syphilis which he did not bring on almost of his own accord. At any rate, he knowingly ran the risk of

[39] *Lettres,* 1841–1866, p. 398.

syphilis as a young man because he said that he was tempted by the most squalid prostitutes. Filth, physical wretchedness, illness and the poorhouse were the things that attracted him and the things he liked in Sarah *l'affreuse Juive:*

Vice beaucoup plus grave, elle porte perruque,
Tous ses beaux cheveux noirs ont fui sa blanche nuque;
Ce qui n'empêche pas les baisers amoureux
De pleuvoir sur son front plus pelé qu'un lépreux.

Elle n'a que vingt ans; la gorge déjà basse,
Pend de chaque côte comme une calebasse,
Et pourtant, me traînant chaque nuit sur son corps,
Ainsi qu'un nouveau-né, je la tette et la mords;

Et, bien qu'elle n'ait pas souvent même une obole
Pour se frotter la chair et pour s'oindre l'épaule,
Je la lèche en silence, avec plus de ferveur
Que Madeleine en feu les deux pieds du Sauveur.

La pauvre créature, au plaisir essoufflée,
A de rauques hoquets la poitrine gonflée,
Et je devine, au bruit de son souffle brutal,
Qu'elle a souvent mordu le pain de l'hôpital [40]

The tone of this poem leaves us in no doubt. In a sense, to be sure, it points to Baudelaire's proud declaration at the close of his life: 'Those who have loved me were people who were generally despised, I might even say despicable if I wanted to flatter the *honnêtes gens.'*

[40] *Vers de jeunesse* which originally appeared in *La Jeune France* and were republished in Eugène Crépet's *Baudelaire.*

88

It is an insolent admission, an implied appeal to the 'hypocritical reader—[his] like and [his] brother.' But we must not forget that it is an *expression* of fact. What is certain is that through Louchette's scraggy body Baudelaire tried to take to himself disease, taints and hideousness. He wanted to assume their burden not out of any feeling of charity, but out of a desire to sear his own flesh. The insolence of the poem is the expression of a reflex reaction: the more the body, which wallowed in filthy pleasures, was soiled and contaminated, the more it became for Baudelaire himself an object of disgust. The more the poet felt that he was *look* and freedom, the more his spirit poured itself out over this diseased bundle of rags. Is it going too far to say that he wanted the syphilis which tortured him all his life, which brought him to dotage and death?

The preceding remarks enable us to understand Baudelaire's famous 'dolorism.' Catholic critics like Du Bos, Fumet and Massin have done much to obscure the question. They have demonstrated by a hundred quotations that Baudelaire called down upon himself the worst forms of suffering. They have quoted the lines from *Bénédiction*:

> *Soyez béni mon Dieu qui donnez la souffrance*
> *Comme un divin remède à nos impuretés.*

But they never seem to have asked themselves whether Baudelaire's sufferings were genuine. On this point Baudelaire's own observations vary a good deal. In 1861 he wrote to his mother:

'The idea of killing myself is absurd isn't it? You'll say: So you're going to leave your old mother all alone.—Lord! if I'm not strictly entitled to do it, I think that the immense amount of suffering I've had to put up with for nearly thirty years makes it excusable.' [41]

He was forty when he wrote this letter which means that the beginning of his misfortunes dated back to his tenth year. This corresponds more or less with an entry in his autobiography:

'After 1830, the school at Lyons, blows, fights with masters and boys, oppressive melancholy.'

It was the famous 'flaw' caused by his mother's second marriage and his letters are filled with a variety of complaints about his state. But we must remember that they always occur in letters to Mme. Aupick. We should not, perhaps, regard this evidence as completely sincere. In any case, when we put extracts like those which follow side by side, we can see that he was capable of changing his mind completely about his position according to the person to whom he was writing. On August 21st, 1860, he wrote to his mother:

'I shall die without having done anything with my life. I once owed 20,000 francs: now I owe 40,000. If I'm unlucky enough to live long enough the debt may be doubled again.' [42]

[41] *Lettres inédites à sa mère*, p. 204.   [42] *ibid.*, p. 204.

We recognize here the theme of the wasted ruined life, the theme of being past redemption; we also recognize the implied reproach over the family council. You would think that the man who wrote in this way must have been in despair. Yet only a month later in the same year—1860—he wrote to Poulet-Malassis:

'When you've found a man who was free at seventeen, had an excessive love of pleasure and no dependents, who embarked on a literary career with 30,000 francs' worth of debts, who at the end of nearly twenty years has only increased his debts by another 10,000 francs and, what is more, who is far from being finished, you must introduce him to me so that I can salute him as my equal.'[43]

This time the tone is one of satisfaction. The man who declares that he is 'far from being finished' is far from thinking that he has done nothing with his life. As for his debts, they were described in the August letter as swelling of their own accord by a sort of malediction; in the September letter, we learn that their growth has been kept within strictly controlled limits thanks to an intelligent economy. Which of the two versions is the true one? Neither, obviously. It is surely significant that Baudelaire should magnify the amount of the debts contracted after 1843 in the letter to his mother and minimize it when writing to Poulet-Malassis. But we can see already that with Mme. Aupick he was anxious to pose as a victim. The letters that he wrote to her are a

[43] *Lettres,* 1841–1866, p. 295.

91

curious mixture of confession and disguised reproach. Most of the time the sense is more or less this: 'Look at the abject state to which you've reduced me.' During the twenty years covered by the correspondence, he repeated the same complaint tirelessly: his mother's marriage and the family council. He declared that Ancelle 'is for [him] the perfect flail and that he is responsible for two-thirds of [his] troubles.' He complained about the education he had received, about the attitude of his mother which was never that of 'a friend,' about the attitude of his stepfather which frightened him. He was afraid of giving the impression that he was happy. If he happened to notice that the tone of his letters was too gay, he hastened to add:

> 'You'll think this letter less miserable than the others. I don't know where my courage comes from: for I have no reason to feel pleased with life.'

In short, the parade of his sufferings clearly had a double purpose. The first was to assuage his rancor—he wanted his mother to feel remorse. The second was more complex. Mme. Aupick represented the judge, represented Good. In her presence he humiliated himself and sought simultaneously condemnation and absolution. But he both hated and respected this Good which he maintained forcibly like a screen in front of him. He hated it because it curbed his freedom, because he had chosen it precisely so that it would be a curb. Those standards were there *in order to be violated,* but they were also there to arouse remorse in the person who violated them. He wished a hundred times that he was quit of them; but his wish was not entirely sincere because if he had been free from them, he would at once have lost the benefits of their protection. Then, as he was unable to look them in the face and by looking them in the face to make them vanish, Baudelaire tried slyly to undermine them from below, to make them appear baneful but without diminishing their absolute value. He adopted an attitude of rancor towards Good. It is a procedure which is frequent in self-punishment. Alexandre quotes a similar case. A man who suffers from a secret love of his mother feels guilty towards his father. He therefore has himself punished by society which is identified with the parental authority, so that the unjust suffering which it inflicts on him diminishes its authority over him and at the same time makes him less guilty. For if Good is less good, Evil becomes less evil. In the same way, the sufferings of which Baudelaire complained were in the nature of an alleviation of his wrongdoing. They established a sort of reciprocity between the sinner and the judge. The sinner had offended the judge, but the judge was the cause of the sinner's unjust sufferings which represented, symbolically, the impossible transcendence of Good in the attempt to achieve freedom. They were credits drawn by Baudelaire on the theocratic universe in which he had chosen to live. In this sense were they not simulated rather than felt? And it is probable that there was not a great deal of difference between a simulated feeling and an affection which was genuinely felt. Yet there remained in these sufferings, which were the product of bad faith, a fundamental lack. They were harassing ghosts, not realities; they were the creation not of events, but of the inner life. They were fed on mists and remained misty; and when, as the result of a shock, Baudelaire made up his mind in 1843 to kill himself, he at once stopped complaining. He explained to Ancelle that it was the objective appreciation of his position which was driving him to suicide and not sufferings which he admitted that he didn't feel.

There was another side to Baudelaire's suffering. It was identical with his pride. The extraordinary letter which he thought of writing to J. Janin and which remained in draft is sufficient to show that from the first he chose to suffer and to suffer more than anyone else:

'You are a happy man. I'm sorry for you, Sir, because it is so easy for you to be happy. A man must have fallen very low to believe himself happy! . . . Ah! so you're happy. Come! If you were to say I am virtuous, I should know that you meant: I suffer less than other people. But not at all. You're happy. So you're easily satisfied? I'm sorry for you, and I feel that my ill-humor is more distinguished than your bliss. I'll go so far as to ask you whether the sights of the earth are sufficient for you. What! You've never wanted to go away simply for a change of scene! I've got sound reasons for feeling sorry for a man who doesn't like death.' [44]

It is a revealing passage. In the first place, it shows that for Baudelaire suffering was not a violent upheaval which followed a shock or a catastrophe, but a permanent state which nothing could increase or diminish. And this state

[44] *Oeuvres posthumes,* 1, pp. 223–233.

corresponded to a sort of psychological tension; it is the degree of this tension which enables us to establish a hierarchy among men. The happy man has lost the spiritual tension and has *fallen*. Baudelaire would never accept happiness because it was immoral. So that a soul's misfortune, far from being the repercussion of an external storm, came from the soul alone; it was its rarest quality. Nothing illustrates more clearly than this the fact that Baudelaire *chose* to suffer. Suffering, he said, is 'nobility.' But it was precisely because it had to be noble that it was unseemly—not in keeping with the phlegmatic nature of the dandy—that it should assume the form of emotion and express itself by cries or tears. When Baudelaire described the man who was unhappy in his heart, he was careful to place the cause of his suffering as far back as possible in his past. 'The sensitive modern man,' who enjoyed his fullest sympathy and whom he introduced in *les Paradis artificiels,* had 'a tender heart wearied by misfortune, but still ready for rejuvenation; we will, if you like, go so far as to admit past faults. . . .' The handsome head of a man, he said in *Fusées,* 'will contain something ardent and sad—spiritual needs, ambitions darkly repressed—the idea of an avenging insensibility . . . finally (so that I may have the courage to admit the extent to which I am modern in aesthetic tastes) *misfortune.*' Hence his 'irresistible sympathy for old women, those beings who have suffered greatly through their lovers, their children and also through their own wrongdoing.'

Why not love them when they were young, when they suffered? Because at that period their sufferings were

95

betrayed by uncontrollable outbursts. They were vulgar. With the passing of time these uncontrollable outbursts were succeeded by a sad equilibrium. It was this that Baudelaire prized above everything else. This state of mind, which should be described as melancholy rather than suffering, appeared in his eyes like an awareness of the human condition. In this sense suffering was the affective aspect of lucidity. 'I'll go so far as to ask you whether the sights of the earth are sufficient for you.' When this lucidity was applied to the human situation, it showed man that he was an exile. He suffered because he was *unsatisfied*.

The function of Baudelaire's particular form of suffering was to express non-satisfaction. 'The sensitive modern man' did not suffer for this or that reason in particular, but in a general way because nothing on this earth could satisfy his desires. People have claimed that this was an appeal to heaven; but, as we have already seen, Baudelaire never had the faith except during a period when he was enfeebled by sickness. His non-satisfaction resulted rather from the consciousness that he suddenly acquired of man's transcendence. Whatever the circumstances, whatever the pleasure offered, man was perpetually beyond them; he transcended them in order to attain other goals and finally in order to possess himself. Except in transcendence in act, the man who is carried along on his course, plunged into a long-term enterprise, scarcely pays attention to the circumstance that he transcends. He does not despise it; he does not announce that he is unsatisfied by it; he uses it as a means, keeping his eyes fixed on the end that he is pursuing. Baudelaire, who was incapable of action and who found himself bounced into short-term enterprises which he used to abandon only to fall into a stupor, discovered in himself, if one can say so, an unfulfilled transcendence. He transcended whatever he saw on his way—that goes without saying—and his eye went beyond what he saw. But the act of transcendence was a movement only in principle; it did not define itself by reference to any end. It lost itself in dreams or, if one prefers, it regarded itself as an end. Baudelaire's non-satisfaction drove him to transcend for the sake of transcending. It was a form of suffering because nothing could overcome or assuage it.

'Anywhere! Anywhere out of the world!'[45] But his continual disappointment was not due to the fact that the objects which he encountered failed to correspond with a given model or to the fact that they were not the instruments which suited his purpose. Since he had transcended them, as it were, in the void, they disappointed him from the very fact that they were. 'They were' meant that they were there so that he could look beyond them. Thus Baudelaire's suffering was the empty exercise of his transcendence in face of the given. His suffering enabled him to adopt the pose of not being of this world. It was another form of his revenge on Good. To the extent, indeed, to which he deliberately submitted to the divine Rule, which was paternal and social, Good enveloped and crushed him. He lay, so to speak, at the bottom of Good as though it were a well. But his transcendence avenged him: even though crushed and bat-

[45] *Les Paradis artificiels:* 'Anywhere out of the World.'

tered by the waves of Good, man is always something else. There was only one thing. If Baudelaire had gone on living his transcendence to the end, it would have led him to challenge Good itself, to move forward to other goals which really would have been his goals. He refused; he stifled the positive impulse; he only wanted to experience it in its negative form of non-satisfaction which was like a continual mental reservation. Through suffering the loop was looped, the system made a closed one. Baudelaire submitted to Good in order to violate it; and if he violated it, it was in order to feel its grip more powerfully; it was in order to be condemned in its name, labelled, transformed into a guilty *thing*. But through suffering he once more escaped condemnation; he discovered once more that he was spirit and freedom. The game was free from risk; he did not challenge Good; he did not transcend it; he simply found it unsatisfying. He was even free from disquiet; he did not consider the possibility of another world with other standards which lay beyond the world he knew. He lived through his non-satisfaction for its own sake; Duty was Duty; this world with its standards was the only one which existed. But the creature he was, by dreaming of impossible escapes, asserted his singularity through his perpetual melancholy, asserted his rights and his supreme value. There was no solution and he did not seek one; he simply became intoxicated by the certainty that he was worth more than the infinite world because he was discontented with it. Everything that was had to be; nothing could be except what was—such was his reassuring starting point. Man dreamt of what could not be, of the unattainable and the contradictory—those were his claims to nobility. That was the completely negative spirituality by which the creature set himself up as a reproach to creation and transcended it. And it was not by chance that Baudelaire saw in Satan the perfect type of suffering beauty. Satan, who was vanquished, fallen, guilty, denounced by the whole of Nature, banned from the universe, crushed beneath the memory of an unforgivable sin, devoured by insatiable ambition, transfixed by the eye of God, which froze him in his diabolical essence, and compelled to accept to the bottom of his heart the supremacy of Good —Satan, nevertheless, prevailed against God, his master and conqueror, by his suffering, by that flame of non-satisfaction which, at the very moment when divine omnipotence crushed him, at the very moment when he acquiesced in being crushed, shone like an unquenchable reproach. In this game of 'whoever loses wins,' it was the vanquished who, *precisely because he was vanquished,* carried off the victory. Proud and vanquished, penetrated by the feeling of his uniqueness in the face of the world, Baudelaire identified himself in the secrecy of his heart with Satan. Human pride has never, perhaps, been pushed farther than this cry, which is always stifled, always repressed, but which echoes all through Baudelaire's work: *'I am* Satan!' But at bottom what was Satan except the symbol of disobedient sulky children who asked that their father's look should freeze them in their singular essence and who did wrong in the framework of Good in order to assert their singularity and to have it consecrated?

The reader will no doubt be a little disappointed with this 'portrait.' Up to the present we have not tried to explain nor have we even mentioned the most obvious and the most celebrated traits of the character whose portrait we set out to paint—his horror of nature, his cult of 'coldness,' his dandyism and his retrograde life, this person who moved forward with his head turned backwards watching time fly as one might watch a road disappearing in a driving mirror. The reader will have looked in vain for some explanation of the very particular form of Beauty which the poet chose and the mysterious charm which makes his poems inimitable. For many people, indeed, Baudelaire is, rightly, purely and simply the author of the *Fleurs du mal;* and they regard any form of research as useless which does not increase our appreciation and understanding of Baudelaire's poetry.

But if the *données* of the empirical character are those which we meet first, they are not the first in the order of formation. They reveal the transformation of a situation by an initial choice. They are the complications of this choice and, to put the matter in a nutshell, in each of them co-exist all the contradictions which disrupt the choice, but the contradictions are reinforced and multiplied by their contact with the diversity of objects in the world. We agree that the choice which we have described—the perpetual see-saw between existence and being—would remain in the air if it were not expressed in a particular attitude towards Jeanne Duval or Mme Sabatier, Asselineau or Barbey d'Aurevilly, a cat, the legion of honor or the poem which Baudelaire happened to be writing. But once it is in contact with reality, it becomes infinitely complicated; each thought, each mood might be described as a 'vipers' tangle,' so varied and conflicting are the meanings which can be attached to them, so great is the extent to which the same act may be desired for mutually destructive reasons. That is why it was desirable to bring to light Baudelaire's choice before going on to examine his behavior.

Baudelaire's biographers and critics have often emphasized his aversion for Nature. They usually attribute its origin to his Christian upbringing and the influence of Joseph de Maistre. The part played by these factors is undeniable and Baudelaire himself invoked them when he wanted to explain his views:

'Most of the errors relating to the beautiful are the outcome of the false conception of morality of the eighteenth century. At that time nature was regarded as the basis, source and type of every possible form of the good and the beautiful. The denial of original sin played no small part in the general blindness of the period. If, indeed, we agree to refer simply to the visible fact, to the experience of all ages and to the *Gazette des Tribunaux,* we shall see that nature teaches nothing or practically nothing, that is to say, it *forces* man to sleep, to drink, to eat and to protect himself as best he can against the inclemency of the weather. It is nature, too, which impels man to kill his fellow, to eat him, to drive him out of his home, to torture him. . . . Crime, for which the human animal acquired a taste in his mother's womb, is in its origins natural. Virtue, on the contrary, is

101

artificial, supernatural, because at all times and in all countries gods and prophets have been necessary to instil it into a brutalized humanity and because man *alone* would have been incapable of discovering it. We do evil without effort, *naturally;* good is always the product of art.' [46]

But this passage, which seems at first decisive, is less convincing when we re-read it. Baudelaire identifies Evil with Nature, and the lines might have been written by the Marquis de Sade. But in order to believe what he says completely, we should have to forget that the true Baudelairean Evil, the Satanic Evil which he evokes a hundred times in his work, is the deliberate product of the will and of Artifice. If therefore there exists a distinguished Evil and a vulgar Evil, it was the vulgarity which must have shocked the poet and not the crime. Moreover, the question is complicated. If, in a number of passages, Nature appears to be identified with original sin, there are many passages in Baudelaire's letters where the expression 'natural' is synonymous with *legitimate* and *just.* I quote one at random, but it would be possible to find a hundred others:

'This idea,' he wrote on August 4th, 1860, 'was the outcome of the most natural and the most filial intention.' [47]

We must therefore conclude that the idea of Nature involved a certain ambivalence. Baudelaire's horror of

[46] *l'Art romantique:* 'Le Peintre de la Vie Moderne,' XI. Eloge du Maquillage, pp. 95–7.
[47] *Lettres inédites à sa mère,* p. 204.

Nature was not so strong that he could not invoke it to justify or defend himself. When we look into it, we shall find in the poet's attitude layers of very different meanings of which the first, which is expressed in the passage from *l'Art romantique* quoted above, is literary and factitious (Maistre's influence on Baudelaire was very much that of a façade: the poet thought it 'distinguished' to claim his patronage) and the last, which is hidden, is merely sensed in the contradiction which we have just mentioned.

What appears to have had a far greater influence on Baudelaire's thought than reading the *Soirées de Saint-Pétersbourg* was the great anti-naturalist current which runs through the whole of the nineteenth century from Saint-Simon to Mallarmé and Huysmans. About 1848 the combined actions of the Saint-Simonians, the Positivists and Marx gave birth to the dream of an anti-nature. The expression 'anti-nature' was actually invented by Comte; and in the Marx-Engels correspondence we find the term *antiphysis*. The doctrines may be different, but the ideal was the same: it was to inaugurate a human order which would be directly opposed to the errors, injustices and blind mechanical forces of the natural World. The introduction of a new factor distinguished this order from the 'City of ends' which Kant put forward at the close of the eighteenth century and which he, too, opposed to a strict determinism. The new factor was work. Man no longer imposed order on the Universe by the pure light of Reason; he did so by work and, oddly enough, by industrial work. The Industrial Revolution of the nineteenth century and the advent of machinism

103

played a far more important part in the origin of this anti-naturalism than the obsolete doctrine of grace. Baudelaire was carried away by the movement. True, he was not much interested in the worker; but work interested him because it was like a *thought* imprinted on matter. He was always attracted by the idea that things are thoughts which have been objectified and, as it were, solidified. In this way he could see his own reflection in them; but natural realities had no significance for him. They meant nothing; and the disgust and boredom which overcame him in face of the vague, mute, disorderly monotony of a landscape were no doubt among the most immediate reactions of his mind.

'You ask me for a poem for your little book. I suppose you mean a poem about *nature,* don't you? About the woods, the great oaks, the verdure, the insects—and probably the sun? But you know perfectly well that I am incapable of getting worked up over plants, and that my whole soul rebels against this peculiar new religion which to my mind will always have something inexpressibly shocking about it for every spiritual being. I shall never believe that *the soul of the god inhabits plant-life,* and even if it did, I shouldn't worry much about it. I should consider my own soul of far more value than the soul of sanctified vegetables.' [48]

Plants, sanctified vegetables—the words show clearly enough his contempt for the insignificance of the vegetable world. He possessed, as it were, a profound intui-

[48] Letter to F. Desnoyer (1855). (*Corres., gén.,* I, pp. 321-3.)

tion of the obstinate, amorphous contingency which is life—it was the precise opposite of work—and he was horrified by it because it seemed to him to reflect the gratuitousness of his own consciousness which he wanted to conceal from himself at any price. As a townsman, he loved the geometrical object which was subjected to human rationalization. Schaunard reports him as saying: 'I find unenclosed water intolerable. I like to see it imprisoned in a yoke between the geometrical walls of a quay.' [49] He wanted work to leave its impress even on the fluidity of water; and since it was impossible to give it a solidity which was incompatible with its natural properties, he would have liked, on account of his horror of its subsidence and its wandering ductility, to imprison it between walls, to give it a geometrical shape. I remember a friend saying to his brother, who was filling a tumbler at the kitchen tap: 'Wouldn't you sooner have *real* water?', and he fetched a jug from the sideboard. The real water was water which was confined and, as it were, rethought by the transparent container and which at once lost its flurried appearance and the scum that came from its promiscuous contact with the sink, with the result that it participated in the spherical, transparent purity which belongs to the work of man. It was not silly, vague, trickling, stagnant, dripping water, but metal collected at the bottom of the jug and humanized by its container. Baudelaire was a townsman and for him *real* water, *real* light and *real* heat meant those which one found in towns and which were already works of art unified by a governing idea. For work had conferred on

[49] *Souvenirs*. Quoted by E. Crépet in *Charles Baudelaire*, p. 31.

them a function and a place in the human hierarchy. A product of nature which has been manufactured and turned into a utensil loses its unjustifiability. A utensil has a right to exist for the man who contemplates it. A carriage in the street or a window pane exist in precisely the manner in which Baudelaire would have wished to exist; they offered him the spectacle of realities which had been called into being by their function and which had appeared in order to fill a gap—were, indeed, produced by the very gap which they were destined to fill. If man becomes frightened in the presence of nature, it is because he feels that he has been trapped in an immense, amorphous, gratuitous existence which completely freezes him by its gratuitousness. He no longer has *his* place anywhere; he is planted on the earth without a goal, without a *raison d'être* like heather or a clump of broom. On the other hand, in the middle of a town he feels reassured because he is surrounded by precise objects whose existence is determined by the part they play and which have a value or a price attached to them like a halo. They show him the reflection of the thing that he wants to be—a *justified* reality. It was precisely to the extent to which he desired to be a thing in the world of Joseph de Maistre that Baudelaire dreamed of an existence in a moral hierarchy where he would have had a function and a value in exactly the same way that a de luxe suitcase or the tractable water in jugs exists in the hierarchy of utensils.

But first and foremost what he called Nature was life. When he spoke of Nature he always mentioned plants and animals. Vigny's *impassible Nature* was the sum total of physico-chemical laws. Baudelaire's was more pervasive. It was a vast, warm, abundant force which penetrated everywhere. He had a horror of this damp warmth, this abundance. This natural prolificness, which knocked off a million copies of the same model, was bound to clash with his love of rarity. He too could say: 'I love the thing that will never be seen a second time.' And he intended it as a eulogy of absolute sterility. What he could not abide about paternity was the continuity of life between the progenitor and his descendants, which meant that the first begetter was compromised by those who came after him and went on leading an obscure and humiliating life in them. This biological eternity seemed intolerable to him: the rare being took the secret of his creation with him to the grave. Baudelaire wanted to be completely sterile because it was the only means of putting a price on himself. He pushed these sentiments so far that he even refused spiritual paternity. He wrote to Troubat in 1866 after a series of articles in praise of Verlaine:

> 'These young men are certainly not without talent, but what follies, what inaccuracies. What exaggerations! What a lack of precision! To tell the truth, they put me in a thorough funk. There's nothing I like so much as being alone.' [50]

The form of *creation* which he lauded to the skies was the opposite of parturition. It did not involve one in compromise. No doubt it was still a form of prostitution, but in this case the cause—the infinite and inexhaustible

[50] Letter of March 5th, 1866. (*Lettres,* 1841–1866, p. 536.)

spirit—remained unchanged after producing its effect. As for the created object, it did not live; it was imperishable and inanimate like a stone or an eternal truth. Yet one must not create with too great an abundance under pain of a *rapprochement* with Nature. Baudelaire often showed his repugnance for Hugo's gross temperament. If he wrote little, it was not on account of impotence. His poems would have seemed less rare to him if they had not been the product of exceptional acts of the mind. Their small number like their perfection was intended to underline their 'supernatural' character; Baudelaire pursued *infecundity* all his life. And in the world which surrounded him, the things which found grace in his eyes were the hard, sterile forms of minerals. In the *Poèmes en prose,* he wrote:

> 'This town stands at the edge of the water. It is said that it is built of marble and that the inhabitants have such a hatred of plant life that they uproot all the trees. It is a landscape which suits (my) taste: a landscape composed of light and minerals with water to reflect them.' [51]

Georges Blin has well said that he 'feared nature as a reservoir of splendor and fecundity and substituted for it the world of his imagination: a metallic universe, a universe which was coldly sterile and luminous.'

It was because for him metal and, in a general way, minerals reflected the image of the mind. One of the results of the limits of our imaginative powers is that all those who, in their endeavors to understand the oppo-

[51] 'Anywhere out of the World.'

sition between the spirit and life and the body, have been driven to form a non-biological image of it, have necessarily had to appeal to the kingdom of inanimate things —light, cold, transparency, sterility. Just as Baudelaire discovered that his own evil thoughts were realized and objectified in 'foul beasts,' so steel—the most brilliant, the most highly polished of metals and the one which offers least grip—always appeared to him to be the exact objectification of his Thought in general. If he felt a tenderness towards the sea, it was because it was a mobile mineral. It was because it was brilliant, inaccessible and cold with a pure and, as it were, an immaterial movement. Because it possessed those forms which succeeded one another, that changed without anything which changed, and sometimes that transparency, that it offered the most adequate image of the spirit. It *was* spirit. Thus Baudelaire's horror of life led him to choose materialization in its purest form as a symbol of the immaterial.

Above everything else, he had a horror of feeling this vast, soft fecundity in himself. Nature, however, was there; needs were there which 'constrained' him to satisfy them. It is sufficient to re-read the passage quoted above to see that it was first and foremost the *constraint* which he hated. A young Russian woman used to take stimulants when she felt like sleeping because she could not bear to give way to the stealthy, irresistible inclination to sink suddenly into sleep, to be nothing more than a sleeping animal. Baudelaire was exactly the same. When he felt nature—the nature which belonged to everybody— rising and taking possession of him like a flood, he went rigid and taut holding his head above the water. The great muddy wave was vulgarity itself. Baudelaire was irritated when he felt inside him the clammy waves which were so unlike the subtle combinations of which he had dreamed; he was irritated above all by the feeling that this soft, irresistible power wanted to make him compliant, make him 'do the same as everybody else.' For the natural elements in us are the opposite of the rare and the exquisite; they are *everybody*. How crazy to eat, sleep and make love like everybody else! Each of us chooses himself those elements of which he can say: 'It's I.' We know nothing of the other elements. Baudelaire chose not to be nature, to be the perpetual jarring refusal of his 'natural self,' the head that stuck out of the water, watching it rise with a mixture of terror and disdain. This free and arbitrary selection, which we operate inside ourselves, constitutes for most of the time what we term our 'style of life.' If you accept your body and allow yourself to be led by it, if you like to surrender to a pleasant feeling of fatigue, to needs, sweat and everything else which makes you the same as other men, if you profess a humanism of nature, your movements will have a sort of roundness and generosity, an easy-going abandon. Baudelaire detested abandon. From dawn till dusk he never let himself go for a moment. His least desires, his most spontaneous *élans* were repressed, filtered, acted rather than lived; they were only allowed to pass when they had been duly transformed into something artificial. That explains in part his cult of appearance and clothes which was designed to conceal a nakedness which would have been too natural, and those fancies, such as painting one's hair green, which sometimes bordered on the ridic-

110

ulous. Inspiration itself found no grace in his eyes, though he probably put his trust in it to some extent.

'In art,' he wrote, 'there is one thing which does not receive sufficient attention. The element which is left to the human will is not nearly so large as people think.'

But inspiration was still a form of nature. It came spontaneously when it wanted. It resembled needs. You had to work on it and transform it. I only believe, said Baudelaire, 'in patient workmanship, in truth expressed in good French and in the magic of the *mot juste.*' Inspiration thus became simple matter to which the poet deliberately applied his poetic technique. His mad desire to find the *mot juste,* as Léon Cladel reminds us, contained a good deal of play acting and a taste for artifice.

'From the first line, nay, at the first line, the first word, you had to begin pulling it to pieces! Was the word really exact? Did it really express in precise form the *nuance* you intended? Be careful! Don't confuse "agreeable" with "amiable," "gracious" with "charming," "forthcoming" with "kind," "seductive" with "provocative," "graceful" with "pleasing." Hoi! These different terms are not synonymous: each of them has a very particular meaning. They belong more or less to the same order of ideas, but they are not saying exactly the same thing! You must never, *never* use one in place of the other. . . . We who are literary—purely literary—workmen must be precise. We must *always* find the expression

111

which is absolutely right or give up writing and finish up as flops. . . . We must hunt and hunt! If the term doesn't exist at all, we must invent it. But let us see first whether it exists or not. And the moment we put our hands on the dictionaries of our own language, they were searched, ransacked, interrogated with rage and love. . . . (Then) came the turn of the dictionaries of foreign language. We began with French-Latin, then Latin-French. A merciless hunt. We've drawn blank with the ancients? Then on to the moderns! And one of the most tenacious of etymologists, to whom most modern languages were as familiar as most of the dead languages, buried himself in English, German, Italian and Spanish dictionaries in pursuit of the elusive, rebellious expression which he always ended by creating if it didn't exist in our language.' [52]

Thus without absolutely denying the fact of poetic inspiration, the poet dreamed of substituting for it pure technique. For this supposedly lazy man regarded work and effort and not creative spontaneity as the attributes of the writer. His taste for the minuteness of artifice enables us to understand how he came to spend such long hours correcting a poem—even when the poem was a very old one and very far removed from his actual mood —rather than write a new one. When he came back, fresh like a stranger, to a poem which was already written and into which he could not enter again, when he experienced the craftsman's joy over changing a word

[52] Quoted by E. Crépet: *Charles Baudelaire,* pp. 242–3.

here and a word there which was derived from the pure pleasure of *arranging,* he felt that he was as far removed as possible from nature, most gratuitous and, as the passage of time had delivered him from the pressure of emotion and circumstance, most free. At the other extreme on the lowest rung of the ladder, his horror of natural needs serves to explain the unfortunate taste which he boasted of for the art of cookery of which he understood nothing and his interminable discussions with the proprietors of cook-shops. He had to disguise his hunger. He did not deign to eat in order to satisfy it. He ate in order to appreciate with his teeth, his tongue and his palate a certain kind of poetic creation. I am prepared to wager that he preferred meats cooked in sauces to grills, preserves to fresh vegetables. This perpetual control, which he exercised over himself, helps us to understand why he made contradictory impressions on people. The ecclesiastical unction, which people frequently remarked on, was the result of his constant supervision of his body; but his cramped, stiff, abrupt gait, which seemed far removed from the gentleness of a prelate, was due to the same cause. In every way he cheated with nature and tried to make it sophisticated. When nature was lulled, he was smooth and smarmy; when he felt that it was awakened, he became rigid all over. He remains the man who said No, who stuffed his poor body into thick clothes, who used a carefully constructed apparatus to hide his poor desires. I am not even sure that this was not one of the sources of his vices. It seems that women excited him mainly when they were clothed. He could not bear the sight of their nakedness. He boasted in

113

Portrait de maîtresse that he had 'long ago reached the climacteric period of the third degree when beauty itself no longer satisfied him unless it were seasoned with perfumes, ornaments, etc.' To judge from a passage in *la Fanfarlo,* an early work which reads like a personal confession, it seems that he began his career in this 'climacteric' period:

'Samuel saw the new goddess of his heart moving towards him in the radiant and sacred splendor of her nakedness.

'What man would not sacrifice half his lifetime to see his dream—his true dream—standing in front of him without so much as a stitch, to see the phantom that he had worshipped in his imagination drop, one by one, the garments intended to protect her from vulgar eyes? But Samuel, seized by an odd caprice, began to shout like a spoilt child:

' "I want Colombine. Give me back Colombine. Give her back to me as she was the evening she drove me mad with her fantastic attire and her actress's bodices!"

'For a moment Fanfarlo was overcome with amazement. But she was perfectly ready to humor the eccentricity of the man whom she had chosen and she rang for Flore. . . . The maid went out of the room. Then, seized with a fresh idea, Cramer flung himself on the bell and roared with a voice of thunder:

' "Hi! don't forget the rouge will you?" ' [53]

[53] *Les Paradis artificiels,* pp. 273–4.

Compare this passage with the famous passage from
Mademoiselle Bistouri:

> ' "I'd like him to come and see me with his instru-
> ments and his overall and even for it to have a bit of
> blood on it!" She spoke with an air of complete can-
> dor, as a sensitive man might say to an actress with
> whom he was in love: "I'd like to see you wearing
> the dress you wore in the famous part you cre-
> ated." ' [54]

—and there seems to be no doubt that Baudelaire was a
fetichist. Does he not himself admit in *Fusées* to

> 'A precocious taste for women. I confused the
> smell of furs with the smell of women. I remember.
> . . . Anyway, I loved my mother for her ele-
> gance.' [55]

Meat disguised, concealed by highly spiced sauces,
water in geometrical basins, the nakedness of women
veiled by furs or by theatrical costumes which still re-
tained a breath of perfume or the gleam of footlights,
inspiration restrained and corrected by hard work—all
this corresponds to so many aspects of his horror of na-
ture and of the commonplace. It takes us a long way
away from the theory of original sin. And when Baude-
laire, through his horror of nakedness and his taste for
hidden, half-seen pleasures and for a titillation which
was purely cerebral, insisted that Jeanne should be fully

[54] *Petits poèmes en prose,* p. 163.
[55] *Fusées.* See also the *Carnet,* Ed. Crépet, p. 110. Note on Agathe.

clothed when making love, we can be sure that he was not thinking of the *Soirées de Saint-Pétersbourg*.

But, as we have seen, his idea of nature was ambivalent. When he was pleading his own cause and wanted to move people by his intentions, he presented his feelings as though they were perfectly *natural* and perfectly legitimate. Here his pen betrayed him. Was it really true that in his heart of hearts he identified nature and sin? Was he really sincere when he made nature the source of crime? No doubt nature stood primarily for conformity, but it is precisely on that account that it is the work of God or, if you prefer, of Good. Nature was the first movement, spontaneity, immediacy, pure uncalculating goodness. It was first and foremost the whole of creation, the hymn which rises up to its Creator. If Baudelaire had been *natural,* he would no doubt have been lost in the crowd but he would also have had a clear conscience, would have carried out effortlessly the divine commandments, would have been completely at home and at his ease in the world. This was the very thing that he did not want. He hated Nature and sought to destroy it *because it came from God* just as Satan sought to undermine creation. Through suffering, non-satisfaction and vice he tried to create for himself a place apart in the universe. His ambition was the solitude which belongs to the accursed and the monster, to 'counter-nature' precisely because Nature is everything and everywhere. His dream of artifice was indistinguishable from his desire of sacrilege. He lied, and he lied to himself, when he identified virtue with an artificial construction. For him Nature was transcendent Good to the extent to which it had become something *given,* a reality which surrounded him and insinuated itself into him without his consent. It revealed the ambiguity of Good which is pure value in so far as it imposes itself and pure *donnée* in so far as it *is* without my having chosen it. Baudelaire's horror of Nature was coupled with a profound attraction towards Nature. The poet's ambivalent attitude is found in those who either will not consent to transcend all the Norms by their choice of themselves or to submit themselves completely to an external system of Morality. Baudelaire himself submitted to Good in so far as it appeared as a Duty which had to be accomplished, but he rejected and scorned it in so far as it was a quality which was given in the universe. And yet it was the same Good which was both of these things because Baudelaire had chosen irrevocably not to choose it.

These observations enable us to appreciate Baudelaire's cult of frigidity. In the first place coldness stood for *himself*—sterile, gratuitous and pure. In contrast to the warm, soft, mucous life, every object which was cold reflected his own image. He had a complex about coldness; he identified it with polished metal and also with precious stones. *Coldness* meant the vast flat spaces without vegetation; and these flat deserts were like the surface of a metal cube or the facet of a jewel. Coldness and paleness merged into one another. White was the color of coldness not merely because snow is white, but chiefly because absence of color was a pretty clear sign of infecundity and virginity. That is why the moon became the emblem of frigidity; the precious stone isolated in the

117

sky turns its chalky steppes towards us and during the coldness of night sheds on the earth a white light which kills the thing it illuminates. The light of the sun appears nourishing; it is golden and thick like bread, and it warms. The light of the moon can be identified with pure water. Through its intermediary, transparency— an image of lucidity—it becomes associated with frigidity. Let us add that the moon with its borrowed brightness and its continual opposition to the sun which lights it, is a tolerable symbol of the satanic Baudelaire illuminated by Good and doing Evil. That is why there remained in this very purity something unhealthy. Baudelaire's coldness was a region where neither spermatazoa, bacteria nor any other germ could exist; it was at once a white light and a transparent liquid, close enough to the limbo of consciousness where the animalcules and solid particles dilute one another. It was the clarity of the moon and of liquid air, the great mineral power which freezes us in winter on the mountain tops. It was avarice and impassibility. Fabre-Luce remarked very truly in his *Écrit en prison* that pity is always warming. Baudelaire's coldness was pitiless: it froze everything it touched.

Of course Baudelaire's attitude simulated this elemental force. With his friends he *was* cold: 'lots of friends, lots of gloves.' He displayed towards them an icy, ceremonious politeness. He did so because he wanted to be sure of killing the warm germs of sympathy, the living waves which tried to pass from them to him. He deliberately surrounded himself with a no man's land where none could penetrate and he saw his own coldness re-

118

flected in the eyes of his fellows. Let us imagine him as a traveller who on a winter's night arrives at an inn covered with ice and snow from outside. He still sees and thinks, but he is no longer aware of his body. It has become insensible.

By a very natural movement Baudelaire projected into the Other the frigidity which belonged to himself. It was at this point that the process became complicated. For the time being it was the Other—the alien consciousness which contemplated and judged—it was the Other who was suddenly invested with the power of freezing. The lunar light became the light of the eye. It was a Medusa look which transfixed and petrified. Baudelaire could scarcely complain of it. Was not the function of the Other's look to transform him into a *thing?* In any case, it was woman alone—and a certain class of woman—whom he invested with this frigidity. He would never have tolerated it in men because to have done so would have been tantamount to admitting that they were superior to him. But woman was an inferior animal, a 'latrine'; she 'is on heat and wants to be poked.' She was the opposite of the dandy. Baudelaire could without danger make her the object of a cult. She could never in any circumstances become his equal. He was in no way taken in by powers with which he invested her. For him she was no doubt, as Royère pointed out, the 'supernatural come to life.' But he knew very well that she was simply a pretext for his dreams precisely because she was completely *other* and impenetrable. At this stage, matters descend to the level of a game. Besides Baudelaire never met a cold woman. Jeanne wasn't cold

119

if we are to believe *Sed non Satiata.* Nor was Mme. Sabatier of whom he complained that she was 'too gay.' He could only realize his desires by resorting to artificial methods of refrigeration with them. He chose to fall in love with Marie Daubrun because she was in love with another man. So that this highly sexed woman adopted, at any rate in her relations with him, an attitude of the iciest indifference. We can see from the letter he wrote to her in 1852 that he enjoyed it in advance:

'A man who says: *I love you,* and who entreats, and a woman who replies: *I, love you? Never! My love belongs to one man only. Bad luck to the person who comes after him. He'd get nothing but my indifference and contempt.* And in order to enjoy the pleasure of looking into your eyes, this same man lets you talk to him about another man, only about another man, only become passionate about him and when thinking of him. For me the result of all these confessions is a very peculiar one. It means that for me you are no longer merely a woman whom I desire, but a woman whom I love for her frankness, for her passion, for her freshness, for her youth, for her folly.

'I've lost a great deal in giving these explanations because you were so downright that I had to submit at once. But you, Madame, have gained a lot from them. You have inspired me with respect and a profound esteem. You must always be the same. Take good care of that passion which makes you so beautiful and so happy.

120

'Come back, I beg of you. I will be gentle and modest in my desires. . . . I don't say that you'll find that I'm no longer in love . . . but you can feel easy in your mind. For me you're the object of a cult and it's impossible for me to sully you.' [56]

This letter tells us a great deal. In the first place, it shows how insincere Baudelaire was. The passionate love which he professed only lasted a few months because that same year he began to write anonymous notes, which were every bit as passionate, to Mme. Sabatier.[57] It was an erotic game and nothing more. People have gone into ectasies over these two love affairs of Baudelaire's; but for anyone who reads between the lines of his letter to Marie Daubrun and his notes to the Présidente, there is something crazy about the repetition of his Platonic adorations. It becomes plainer still when we turn to the famous poem, *Une nuit que j'étais près d'une*

[56] *Corres. gén.*, 1; pp. 101–2. (Crépet assigns this letter to the year 1847. See his note *ibid.*, p. 100. *Tr.*)

[57] In the second case the process was the same. First of all Baudelaire was careful to choose a woman who was happy, loved and not free. With her as with the other he proclaimed the liveliest admiration for the official lover. In both cases he worshipped the woman 'as a Christian [worshipped] his God.' But as Mme. Sabatier seemed to be easier game and as, after all, she ran the risk of falling into his arms, he remained anonymous. In this way he was able to enjoy his idol in comfort, love it in secret and be overwhelmed by its disdainful indifference. She had scarcely given herself to him when he made off. She no longer interested him and he could not go on with the game. The statue had come to life, the cold woman had grown warm. It even seems probable that he had a fiasco with her so that his impotence compensated for the coldness which suddenly failed in the Présidente.

affreuse Juive, which according to Crarond goes back to the time of Louchette and in which Baudelaire, who did not yet know either Marie or Mme. Sabatier, outlines the theme of feminine duality and describes himself dreaming of the frigid angel while lying beside the passionate demon:

> *Je me pris à songer, près de ce corps vendu*
> *A la triste beauté dont mon désir se prive . . .*
> *Car j'eusse avec ferveur baisé son noble corps . . .*
> *Si quelque soir, d'un pleur obtenu sans effort*
> *Tu pouvais seulement, ô reine des cruelles!*
> *Obscurcir la splendeur de tes froides prunelles.*

It is therefore an *a priori* graph of Baudelaire's sensibility which for a long time functioned in the void and only later achieved concrete realization. The frigid woman was a sexual incarnation of the judge:

> 'When I do something really foolish, I say to myself: Heavens! if she knew! When I do a good action, I say to myself: That's something which has brought me closer to her in spirit.' [58]

Her coldness is a sign of her purity: she is free from original sin. At the same time she is identified with an alien consciousness and stands for incorruptibility, impartiality, objectivity. Her look is also the look of clear water and melted snow. It shows no sign of irritation or surprise. It restores everything to its proper place and *thinks* the world and Baudelaire in the world. There is no doubt that this frigidity, which was so carefully culti-

[58] Letter of August 18th, 1857. (*Corres. gén.*, 2, p. 88.)

vated, recalled the icy severity of the mother who catches her child just when he is 'doing something silly.' But, as we have seen, it was not so much the incestuous love of his mother which made him seek authority in the women he desired; his need of authority, on the contrary, led him to transform his mother like Marie Daubrun and the Présidente into a judge and an object of desire. He wrote of Mme. Sabatier that:

> *Rien ne vaut la douceur de son autorité.*

He recognized that, by a sort of balancing movement, he thought of her in the midst of his orgies:

> *Quand chez les débauchés l'aube blanche et vermeille*
> *Entre en société de l'Idéal rongeur,*
> *Par l'opération d'un mystère vengeur*
> *Dans la brute assoupie un ange se réveille.*

It will be seen that it is a question here of an *operation*. He reveals the mechanism in another passage:

> 'The thing that makes one's mistress dearer to one is an orgy with other women. What she loses in sensual pleasure, she gains in adoration. The knowledge that he is in need of forgiveness makes a man more amiable.'

We find in this passage another common characteristic of pathological Platonism—the sick man who worships a respectable woman from a distance, who evokes her image when he is engaged in the basest occupations, when he is in the lavatory or washing his genital organs. It is then that she makes her appearance and gazes at him in silence with an expression of severity. He manipulated this obsession as he pleased. It was when he was lying beside the *affreuse Juive,* dirty, bald and pox-ridden, that he chose to conjure up the Angel. The personality of the Angel varied; but whoever the woman might be whom he had selected to perform this function, there was always *someone* who was looking at him—no doubt at the very moment of the orgasm. So that he no longer knew whether he described this face as chaste and severe in order to increase the pleasures he enjoyed with harlots, or whether his hurried connection with them merely served to evoke the chosen woman and put him in contact with her. In any case, this large, frigid, silent, motionless form was for Baudelaire the expression in erotic terms of the social sanction. It resembled the mirrors used by certain men of refinement to reflect their pleasures: it enabled Baudelaire to see himself while in the act of making love.

But more directly still his love of her was guilty because she didn't love him in return. He felt even more guilty if he desired and smirched her. Her very frigidity was a symbol of the *forbidden thing;* and if he swore with the most solemn oaths to respect her, it was so that his desires should become even greater crimes. Here once more we meet wrongdoing and sacrilege. The woman is there. She crosses the room with that indolent, majestic step of which Baudelaire was so fond and which in itself stood for indifference and freedom. She is unaware of Baudelaire or practically so; if she happens to look at him, he seems to her to be *just anyhow.* He passes across her field of vision:

124

Comme passe le verre au travers du soleil.

Sitting far away from her in silence, he feels that he is insignificant and transparent—an object. But at the very moment at which the eyes of the beautiful creature put him in the place in the world to which her passionless look assigns him, he makes his escape. The two 'simultaneous postulations' are suddenly present together in his soul; he is invaded by the double pressure of those two inseparables—Good and Evil.

At the same time, the frigidity of the beloved spiritualizes Baudelaire's desires and transforms them into *voluptés.* We have already seen the sort of restrained pleasure—pleasure leavened by the spirit—which he sought. It was, as we have said, a matter of the merest touch. Such were the pleasures that he promised himself in the letter to Marie Daubrun. He would desire her in silence and his desire would envelop her completely at a distance without leaving a mark, without her even noticing it:

> 'You can't prevent my mind from hovering round your arms, your lovely hands, your eyes where your whole life resides, the whole of your adorable physical person.'[59]

Thus the coldness of the beloved object realized what Baudelaire sought to procure for himself by every means: the solitude of desire. The desire which hovers at a distance round beautiful, unresponsive flesh, which is no more than a visual caress, derives pleasure from itself

[59] *Corres. gén.,* I, p. 102.

because it is unknown and unrecognized. It is essentially sterile; it rouses no response on the part of the woman who is loved. We know the communicative desire of which Proust speaks in describing Swann and which appears with such suddenness that for a moment the woman who is desired remains completely damp and shattered by it. It was precisely this that Baudelaire abominated. It arouses sexual excitement. Little by little it animates and warms the icy nakedness of the object of desire; it is a warm, fertile, communicative desire which has affinities with the warm abundance of nature. Baudelaire's desire was essentially sterile and *without consequence.* From the moment of its origin, he was its master because 'la froide majesté de la femme stérile' could only arouse a cerebral love which was represented rather than experienced. It was more the will to desire, a phantom desire, than a reality.

In the first place, it was this mysterious void which Baudelaire enjoyed because it did not in any way compromise him. And since the object of desire did not take any notice of it, this simulated excitement, which was acted rather than experienced, did not involve him. He remained alone, imprisoned in his onanist's greed. Besides, if he had had to make love to one of these inaccessible beauties—he was careful not to do so because he preferred the nervous irritation of desire to its satisfaction —it would have been on the express condition that she remained to the very end like a block of ice. 'The woman one loves,' he once wrote, 'is the one who doesn't get any fun out of it.' He would have been horrified at the idea of giving pleasure. As long as the statue remained marble, the sexual act was, so to speak, *neutralized*. Baudelaire only had relations with himself; he remained as solitary as the child who masturbates. The voluptuous feelings which he experienced were not the source of any external event; he *gave* nothing; he made love to a block of ice. Because she didn't remain a block of ice but showed that she had a body which was too sensitive and a temperament which was too generous, the Présidente lost her lover in a single night.

But here again, as with the idea of the 'natural,' there is ambivalence. The sexual act with the frigid woman certainly represented an act of sacrilege, the smirching of Good which nevertheless left it as pure, as virginal and as unpolluted as before. It was the *blank* sin, sterile, without memory, without effect, which vanished into the air at the very moment it was committed and yet realized the unalterable eternity of the law, the eternal youth and the eternal disponibility[60] of the sinner. But love's white magic did not exclude black magic. As we have seen, through his failure to transcend Good, Baudelaire slyly set to work to depreciate its value from below. Thus the masochism, which is apparent in his cult of frigidity, was accompanied by sadism. The frigid woman was a judge who was feared, but she was also a

[60] In French, *disponibilité*. Another example of the way in which Existentialist philosophers have given a special meaning to a common word. For this reason, I have preferred a literal translation to the more common 'availability.' M. Sartre appears to have adopted this word from the writings of M. Gabriel Marcel. 'Disponibility' is a favorite category of M. Marcel's. For example, according to this philosopher, man cannot enter into the right relation with God unless he is 'disponible.' *Tr.*

victim. If with Baudelaire there were three participants in the sexual act, if the idol appeared to him at the time when he surrendered to his vices in the company of prostitutes, it was not only because he needed some one who would despise and judge him; it was also because he wanted to flout her. It was she whom he 'got' when he penetrated into his hired companion. He deceived and smirched her. It might be said that through his horror of direct action on the universe, Baudelaire turned to magic influences, that is to say, influences which operate at a distance—no doubt because they compromised him less. The frigid woman thus became the *decent woman* whose decency was even a little ridiculous and whose husband was unfaithful to her with harlots. That, at least, is what the curious *Fanfarlo* suggests. Here coldness becomes clumsiness, inexperience and, when the woman who loves forces herself to indulge in erotic practices which are repugnant to her in order to keep her husband, her coldness is not free from obscenity. In the same way, the 'blank' sexual act, the empty possession which takes place almost at a distance and without sullying the woman 'who doesn't get any fun out of it,' is sometimes transformed into a pure and simple rape. Like Mme. Aupick, like Marie Daubrun, all Baudelaire's heroines were in love with someone else. It was the guarantee of their coldness; and the fortunate rival was endowed with all the virtues. In *la Fanfarlo*, M. de Cosmelly is 'noble, upright.' We are told of his 'extremely handsome features'; he assumes 'with everybody a commanding air which is at once affable and irresistible.' In *l'Ivrogne,* a sketch for a play which came to nothing, the drunkard's wife is in love with 'a man who is young, quite well off, whose social standing is higher than her own, who is upright and admires her virtue.' In *la Fanfarlo,* this produces a curious plot. Mme. de Cosmelly is flouted by her husband with the Fanfarlo, is flouted a second time—at her own request—with the same creature by Baudelaire himself under the name of Cramer. The subject of the story, which is barely disguised, is the decent woman who is ridiculed and violated by magic in the form of a magnificent strumpet. It is the story of coldness humiliated. But in *l'Ivrogne,* 'our workman will clutch joyfully at the pretext of his own excited jealousy to conceal from himself the real reason of his anger with his wife—her resignation, her gentleness, her patience, her virtue.' Hatred of good is clearly apparent in this passage. It will drive the drunkard to an act of straightforward rape. In the version of 1854 (letter to Tisserand) murder is somewhat absurdly substituted for rape at the last moment as a cloak for the real theme:

'Here's the setting of the crime. Note carefully that it is premeditated. The man arrives first at the meeting place. It was he who had chosen the place. It's Sunday evening. A dark road or open country. In the distance the sound of a dance hall. A sinister, melancholy stretch of country near Paris. A love scene as sad as possible between the man and the woman. He wants to be forgiven. He wants her to let him live and return to her. Never has he seen her looking more beautiful. . . . He grows tender and his tenderness is genuine. He is almost in love with

129

her again. He desires her: he pleads with her. Her pallor and her thinness make her more interesting and act almost as a stimulant. The public must guess what it's all about. In spite of the fact that the poor woman also feels something of her old affection stirring, she refuses to surrender to this brutal passion in such a spot. Her refusal irritates the husband who attributes her chastity to the existence of an adulterous passion or to the prohibition of a lover. "We must make an end of it. But I shall never have the courage. I couldn't do it myself." ' [61]

We know the rest. He sends his wife to the end of the road where there is a well and she falls into it. 'If she escapes so much the better. If she falls in, it's God who condemns her.'

We can see the symbolic richness of this fantasy. The crime is premeditated. It is this that sets the general tone of the relations between Baudelaire, the drunkard, and his wife (his mother, Marie Daubrun, etc.). Everything that follows is therefore seen against a background of crime. With the result that the tenderness of the drunkard is poisoned the moment it comes into being. He is the sadist weeping—a thing that often happens—over his victim. But besides this, the figure of Baudelaire-Drunkard tackles the frigid woman by *asking her forgiveness*. The love theme is therefore the *blank theme* of masochism. The pallor and the thinness of the woman excite him (theme of frigidity and the *affreuse Juive*).

[61] *Corres. gén.*, pp. 252–3.

We know that to Baudelaire thinness appeared 'more obscene' than plumpness. This is the moment of transition to sadism. The drunkard wants to violate this coldness, to smirch it and through the woman to get at the lover who is more fortunate than himself and who stands for morality. (He has 'forbidden' her to recommence sexual intercourse with her husband.) At the same time, he wants to finish off (rape=murder) the decomposition of the body which is already apparent from its thinness. He wants to force her gentleness, her chastity to turn into something obscene; he wants to have this woman here and now at the crossroads as though she were the lowest whore (and, we notice, he wants to have her fully dressed—we shall meet the theme of fetichism again in *la Fanfarlo*). Because she refuses, he kills her. Or rather, since he does not possess the necessary strength for direct action, he puts the burden of getting rid of her on chance and magic. (Theme of impotence and sterility: you do not act yourself; you make someone else act). The crime is used to conceal the rape both because there is affective equivalence between them and because Baudelaire was frightened of himself. Rape was too obviously erotic, but the crime hides the sexual content of the story. He kills the woman in order to get inside her and sully her, to get at the Good in her. But he muffs this act of possession while she is still alive, and she dies behind him in the dark—dies a death that he has merely prepared by words. This fantasy haunted Baudelaire for a long time. This sly crime did not satisfy him entirely because Asselineau tells us that he imagined another:

131

'Baudelaire described (to Rouvière) one of the principal scenes of the part, where the drunkard, after killing his wife, experienced a return of tenderness and a desire to violate her. Rouvière's mistress protested against such an appalling situation. "Ah! Madam," said Baudelaire, "everyone would do the same in the circumstances. And those who aren't like that are oddities." ' [62]

This story may be earlier than the letter to Tisserand and Baudelaire may, through fear of the theatrical censorship and also no doubt to give the scene action, have altered the moment at which desire came into being, so that the woman would still be *alive*. That is likely enough because in other places he speaks of a different ending—indirect murder, though the presence of the corpse was necessary if the temptation to commit necrophilia were to have any meaning. Originally therefore the drunkard strangled or stabbed his wife and then violated her. The insensibility, the sterility and the inaccessibility of the frigid woman are interpreted here in their extreme sense and are fully realized: in the end the frigid woman is the corpse. It is in the presence of the corpse that sexual desires assumes its most criminal and its loneliest form. What is more, disgust at this dead flesh will at the same time fill him with a profound sense of the void, will make him more the master of his actions, more artificial and will, so to speak, 'cool him down.' Thus frigidity, which begins with sterilization by coldness, discovers in

[62] Asselineau, *Recueil d'ancedotes* (published for the first time in full by E. Crépet in *Charles Baudelaire*, pp. 293–4.)

the end its true climate which is death. Its meaning
varied as Baudelaire himself oscillated between mas-
ochism and sadism, between the lunar metal—icy and
incorruptible—and the corpse which was losing its animal
warmth. Absence of life or destruction of life—these are
the extreme limits between which the Baudelairean *spirit*
operated.

After these observations, there remains little to say
about Baudelaire's famous dandyism. The reader will
be able to work out for himself its relation with Baude-
laire's anti-naturalism, his cult of artificiality and fri-
gidity. There are nevertheless one or two points which
must be mentioned. In the first place, Baudelaire himself
noted that dandyism was a moral code based on effort:

> 'For those who are at once its priests and victims,
> all the complicated material conditions to which they
> must submit, from their dress, which must be irre-
> proachable at every hour of the day and night, to the
> most dangerous tricks of sport, are nothing but a
> form of gymnastics which is designed to fortify the
> will and discipline the spirit.' [63]

He himself used the word Stoic in this context. He
inflicted these minute, finicky rules on himself primarily
in order to put the brake on his bottomless freedom.
Through obligations which were constantly renewed, he
concealed his own inner gulf from himself. He was a
dandy first and foremost because he was afraid of him-
self. It was the *ascesis* of the Cynics and the Stoics. It

[63] *l'Art romantique.* 'Le Peintre de la Vie Moderne—IV Le Dandy.'
p. 90.

will be seen that by its gratuitousness, by the free creation of values and obligations, dandyism resembled the choice of a moral system. It seems that at this level, Baudelaire satisfied the transcendental element in himself of which he had been aware from the first. But it was a spurious satisfaction. Dandyism was only the pale image of the absolute choice of unconditional Values. In fact the dandy remained within the limits of traditional Good. He was no doubt gratuitous, but he was also completely inoffensive. He did not upset any of the established laws. He wanted to be useless and no doubt he did not *serve;* but he didn't do any harm either. And the ruling class always preferred a dandy to a revolutionary just as the bourgeoisie in the reign of Louis-Philippe was more ready to tolerate the extravagences of Art for Art's sake than the *littérature engagée* of Hugo, Sand and Pierre Leroux. It was a childish game which adults watched indulgently. The rules were simply a few extra obligations which Baudelaire took on in addition to those imposed on him by Society. He spoke of them insolently and emphatically, but also with a smile at the corner of his mouth. He didn't want people to take him absolutely seriously.

But at a rather deeper level, these strict and useless rules represented his ideal of effort and constructiveness. Baudelaire's nobility and his greatness as a man are due in a large measure to his horror of drift. Flabbiness, abandonment and slackness seemed to him to be unforgivable sins. You needed to withhold yourself, to keep a grip on yourself, to concentrate your energies. He observed after Emerson that 'the hero is the man who is immovably centred.' He admired Delacroix's 'conciseness and a sort of unostentatious intensity which are the inevitable result of the concentration of the whole of his spiritual powers on a given point.' We know Baudelaire well enough by now to understand the meaning of these maxims. Although he lived in an age of determinism, he possessed from birth an intuition that the spiritual life was not something given, but something which created itself. And his reflective lucidity enabled him to formulate the ideal of self-possession. Man was really himself, in good as in evil, when tension reached its extreme point. It was always a question of the same effort towards recovery while remaining 'different.' To hold oneself in, to put a bridle on oneself, was a way of bringing into being beneath one's fingers and the reins the *Self* that one wanted to possess. From this point of view, dandyism was an episode in a venture in which Baudelaire was continually coming to grief; he was Narcissus trying to mirror himself in his own waters and catch his reflection. Lucidity and dandyism were simply the forms assumed by the couple 'executioner-victim,' in which the executioner tried in vain to detach himself from the victim and to discover his own image in its shattered features. At this point, the effort to divide himself into two assumed its most acute form. His aim was to exist for himself as an object, to dress up in all his finery and paint himself in order to be able to take possession of the object, to remain long in contemplation of it and, finally, to melt into it. It was this that gave Baudelaire the appearance of perpetual tenseness; abandonment was as unknown to him as spontaneity. Nothing was farther removed from vagueness of soul than his spleen. On the contrary, it was the sign of a virile non-satisfaction, an arduous and voluntary act of transcendence. Blin has well said:

> 'Baudelaire's merit is to have given a juster resonance to *malaise* by stripping it of its stale formulas. . . . The novelty lies in presenting aspiration as a "tension of spiritual forces" and not as a form of dissolution. . . . What finally distinguishes Baudelaire from Romanticism is that he transformed *malaise* into a principle of conquest.'[64]

Thus in his case psychic becoming could only take the form of incessantly *working on himself*. He went out of his way to restrain himself so that his disponibility would always be at its peak. For Baudelaire, disponibility was not Gide's surrender to the moment, but a fighting attitude. There was only one thing. The aim of these internal operations could never be to bring a useful enterprise to a successful conclusion; they had to remain gratuitous. Nor must they lead him to question the validity of the moral system of theocracy. They therefore had to be confined to the pure gratuitousness of dandyism.

There was another point. Dandyism, as Baudelaire did not fail to observe, was a ceremonial. It is, he said, the cult of the ego and he proclaimed himself its 'priest and its victim.' But at the same time and by an apparent contradiction, he claimed through dandyism to become a

[64] Op. cit., pp. 81–2.

member of a very exclusive artistocracy 'which is all the more difficult to destroy because it will be founded on the most precious, the most indestructible faculties and on those divine gifts which money and work cannot confer.' And dandyism became 'an institution outside the law [which] has severe laws of its own to which all its subjects must submit.' [65]

We must not be misled by the *collective* nature of this institution. For if, on the one hand, Baudelaire presents it as though it emanated from a *caste,* on the other, he returns on several occasions to the fact that the dandy was a *déclassé*. In reality, Baudelaire's dandyism was a personal reaction to the problem of the social position of the writer. In the eighteenth century, the existence of an hereditary aristocracy had simplified everything. Whatever his origin, whether he happened to be a bastard, the son of a cutler or of a president of the High Court, the professional writer had direct access to the aristocracy over the heads of the bourgeoisie. The nobility might order him a pension or a beating, but he was immediately dependent on it and looked to it for his income as well as for his social standing. He was, so to speak, 'aristocratized.' The aristocracy bestowed on him a little of its *mâna*. He shared its idleness and the fame which he hoped to win was a reflection of the immortality which its hereditary title confers on a royal family. When the nobility collapsed, the writer was completely bewildered by the fall of his protectors and had to look for some fresh form of justification. His connection with the sacred caste of priests and nobles really had made him into a *déclassé*. In other words, he

[65] *l'Art romantique,* p. 91.

had been torn from the middle classes into which he was born, cleansed of his origins and nourished by the aristocracy without, however, being taken to its bosom. He had depended for his employment and the satisfaction of his material needs on a superior and inaccessible society which, idle and parasitic itself, had remunerated him for his work by capricious gifts which had borne no visible relation to the work that he had actually done. He belonged, however, by family ties, friendships and the mode of his daily life to a bourgeoisie which no longer had the means to justify him. The result was that he had come to feel that he was a person apart, in the air and rootless, a Ganymede who had been carried off in the claws of an eagle; and he had the continual feeling that he was superior to his milieu. But after the Revolution the bourgeoisie itself assumed power. It was this class which should logically have conferred on the writer a new dignity; but this could only have been done if the writer had consented to return to the bourgeois fold. Now there could be no question of that. In the first place, two hundred years of royal favors had taught the writer to despise the bourgeoisie; but, what was more important, as a parasite on a class which was itself parasitic, he had been accustomed to regard himself as a *clerc*, cultivating pure thought and pure art. If he returned to his own class, he would undergo a radical change. If the bourgeoisie was, indeed, a class of oppressors, it was not parasitic; it despoiled the worker, but it worked with him. The creation of a work of art inside bourgeois society was equivalent to providing a service. The poet was expected to place his talent at the disposal of his class in the same way as a barrister or an engineer. He was expected to help it towards self-awareness and contribute his share to the development of the myths which enabled it to oppress the proletariat. In exchange, bourgeois society would invest the writer with a special aura. But he would lose on the deal. He would sacrifice his independence and his claim to superiority. He would, to be sure, be a member of an *élite,* but there was also an *élite* of doctors and an *élite* of solicitors. The hierarchy was constituted inside the class in accordance with its social utility; and the guild of artists would take a secondary position just above the teaching profession.

This was what the majority of writers could not accept. For one Émile Augier, who was exemplary in carrying out the terms of his contract, there was a vast number of malcontents and rebels. What could be done about it? It never entered anyone's head, of course, to demand justification from the proletariat, which would have produced just as real a *déclassement,* but in the opposite direction. No one had the courage either to demand the great free solitude, the choice of oneself in anguish which was to be the lot of a Lautréamont, a Rimbaud, a van Gogh. A few like the Goncourts and Mérimée curried favor with an aristocracy of parvenus and endeavored, without any real satisfaction, to play the same role among the nobility of the Napoleonic period that their predecessors had played among the courtiers of Louis XV. But the great majority of them attempted a symbolical *déclassement.* Flaubert is a case in point. Although he led the life of a wealthy provincial bourgeois, he laid it down as an *a priori* condition that he should escape from the bourgeoisie; and he achieved a symbolical break with his class which seems like a pale reflection of the real break produced in the eighteenth century by the introduction of the bourgeois writer into Mme. Lambert's salon and his friendship with the Duc de Choiseul. This break was *acted* without a moment's respite by symbolic attitudes. Clothes, food, manners, conversation and taste had of necessity to simulate a separation which without constant vigilance might well have passed unnoticed. In this sense Baudelaire's cult of being different reappeared in a Flaubert or a Gautier. But the symbolic *déclassement,* which might easily have led to freedom and madness, had to be accompanied by an equally mythical integration into a society which resembled the return of the vanished aristocracy. This meant that the collectivity into which the artist introduced himself had to reproduce the characteristics of the parasitic class which in earlier times had given him his special aura; and the new society also had to be firmly established outside producer-consumer circles on a basis of non-productive activity. Flaubert chose to stretch out his hand across the centuries to Cervantes, Rabelais and Virgil. He knew that in a hundred, a thousand years' time, other writers would come who would hold out their hands to him. He imagined, naïvely, that they would be like the author of *Don Quixote* who was the parasite of monarchist Spain, the author of *Gargantua* who was the parasite of the Church, and the author of the *Aeneid* who was the parasite of the Roman Empire. It never even entered his head that the very function of the writer might change in the course of the centuries to come, and with the naïve optimism which accompanied his gloomiest pronouncements, he worked out a free-masonry which, he felt sure, had begun with the first man and would finish with the last. This discreet society, which was largely composed of the dead and of unborn children, was completely satisfying for the artist. First and foremost it was founded on what Durkheim called 'mechanical solidarity.' In effect, the living artist bore within himself, and represented at every moment of his life, the whole corpus of artists in the same way that the gentleman carries about with him everywhere and represents in everybody's eyes his family and his ancestors. But in the latter case honor is a bond of organic solidarity; the nobleman has a variety of precise obligations towards his dead ancestors and his future descendants. They exist through him; he is responsible for them and can make or mar them. Virgil, on the contrary, had no need of Flaubert; his glory could very well dispense with any individual co-operation. In the mythical society chosen by the writer, all the members are neighbors without engaging in any communal action. Let us be clear about it. They are all side by side like the dead in a cemetery; and, since they are dead, there is nothing particularly surprising about it. But this college which imposed no obligations nevertheless poured out its gifts upon Flaubert. It did, indeed, raise literary activity to a social function. The immortal dead, who for the most part had lived in solitude, unrest and astonishment, who had never quite managed to see themselves either as artists or writers and who like anyone else had died in a state of uncertainty, were hailed from without—because they belonged to the *past* and their lives appeared as destinies—

141

by the title of poet which they had certainly been anxious to win without ever being sure whether or not they had won it; and instead of regarding it as the goal of their efforts, they had looked on it as a *vis a tergo,* a character. They did not write in order to become writers; they wrote because they already were writers. As soon as we identify ourselves with them, and live mythically in their society, we feel convinced that we, too, possess this character. So that Flaubert's own occupation, far from being the result of a gratuitous and perilous choice, appeared to him to be the manifestation of his own nature. But since it was also a question of a society of the elect, of a monastic order, the writer's nature seemed to him to be like the exercise of a priestly office. Every word that Flaubert put down on paper was like a moment of the Communion of Saints. Through him Virgil, Rabelais and Cervantes came back to life and continued to write with his pen. Thus through the possession of the strange quality which was at once predisposition and priestly office, nature and sacred function, Flaubert tore himself away from the bourgeoisie and was submerged in a parasitic aristocracy which satisfied him. He concealed from himself his gratuitousness and his unjustifiable freedom of choice. He replaced the fallen nobility by a spiritual college and he safeguarded his mission as a *clerc.*

There can be no doubt that Baudelaire, too, chose to enter the same college. A hundred, a thousand times in his writings he speaks of the 'poet' and the 'artist.' He managed to have himself justified and consecrated by the writers of the past. He even went farther than this by forming a friendship with a dead poet. The real purpose of his long liaison with Edgar Poe was to procure his elevation to the mystic order. It has been said that he was attracted by the disturbing resemblances between the American poet's life and his own. That is true, but this identity of fate only interested him *because Poe was dead*. If he had been alive, the author of *Eureka* would have been no more than a vague body like his own. How could two unjustifiably gratuitous beings have been placed side by side? Once he was dead, however, his portrait assumed its final form and its features became clear. It was perfectly natural to describe him as poet and martyr; his existence had become a destiny; his misfortunes seemed to be the result of predestination. It was then that the resemblances acquired their full value; they transformed Poe, as it were, into an image in Baudelaire's past, into something like the John the Baptist of an accursed Christ. Baudelaire leant over the depths of the years, over the distant, hated America, and suddenly he caught sight of his own reflection in the gray waters of the past. That's what he *is*. At once his existence was consecrated. He differed in one respect from Flaubert. He did not need a complete college of artists (though his poem, *les Phares,* is like a census of his own spiritual order). He was the exasperated individualist and there again he *chose*. The chosen one became the representative of the whole *élite*. A glance at the celebrated prayer in *Fusées* is sufficient to prove that Baudelaire's relations with Poe were also associated with the Communion of Saints:

143

'Say a prayer every morning to God, the reservoir
of all power and all justice, to my father, to Mariette
and Poe as intercessors.'

This means that in Baudelaire's mystic soul the lay com-
munity of artists had assumed a deeply religious value.
It had become a church. Its parasitic character, which
Baudelaire regretted and tried to reconstitute, was that of
an ecclesiastical aristocracy. And each member of this
aristocracy found in another member (or, according to
Baudelaire's mood, in all the other members), a sanctified
image of himself and a guardian angel.

But this spiritual college could not satisfy the poet
completely. First of all by a contradiction, which was in-
herent in his initial choice, he had scarcely received the
label he desired before he was dissatisfied. He was, and
at the same time he was not, the Poet. If he saw himself
lonely and wretched, crushed by the immense responsi-
bility of his own choice, he quickly sought to return to a
monastic order; but as soon as he was received at the
monastery, he wanted to get away again. He refused to
be no more than *a* monk among other monks. In a sense
the artist's activity did not seem to him to be gratuitous
enough. The painter and the writer had a passion to see
and describe which still seemed to him to be plebeian.
This is apparent in a passage in his study of Constantin
Guys:

'I have told you that I find it repugnant to call him
a pure artist and that he defended himself against the
title with a majesty mixed with an aristocratic feeling
of shame. I would willingly describe him as a *dandy*

and should have a number of sound reasons for doing so; for the word *dandy* implies a quintessential character and a subtle sense of the whole moral mechanism of the world; but on the other hand, the dandy aims at insensibility and it is at that point that M. Guys, who is dominated by an insatiable passion to see and feel, voluntarily parts company with dandyism.' [66]

To anyone who reads between the lines, it is clear that dandyism represented a higher ideal than poetry. It is a question of a society of the second degree conceived on the model of the society of artists drawn up by Flaubert, Gautier and the theorists of Art for Art's sake. From the model it borrows the ideas of gratuitousness, mechanical solidarity and parasitism; but it increases the difficulty of the conditions of admission to the association. The essential characteristics of the artist are exaggerated and pushed to their farthest limit. The exercise of the artist's profession, which still seems too utilitarian, becomes the pure ceremonial of dress; the cult of beauty, which produces stable and lasting works of art, changes into love of elegance because elegance is ephemeral, sterile and perishable. The creative act of the painter or the poet is emptied of its substance and assumes the form of an act which is strictly gratuitous—in Gide's sense—and even absurd; artistic invention is transformed into mystification; the passion to create is frozen into insensibility.

At the same time, Baudelaire's taste for death and decadence, which looked forward to Barrès and which was

[66] *l'Art romantique,* p. 61.

associated with his cult of individuality, drove him to refuse what Flaubert demanded. He did not want a society which would last as long as the human species. The society he wanted could only enjoy the cachet of rarity and uniqueness if it were doomed to disappear in the very heart of humanity. That is why dandyism was 'the last gleam of heroism in periods of decadence . . . a setting sun.' In short, Baudelaire instituted an order of regulars which was above the aristocratic but secular society of artists and which represented pure spirituality; and he claimed to belong to both societies at the same time, though the second was no more than the quintessence of the first. Thus this recluse, who feared solitude, settled the question of social relations by imagining magic relations which made possible contact between isolated beings, the majority of whom were dead. He created the parasite of parasites—the dandy who was the parasite of a class of oppressors; beyond the artist, who still sought to create, he projected a social idea of absolute sterility in which the cult of the self was identified with the suppression of oneself. That is why J. Crépet could rightly say that 'suicide is the supreme sacrament of dandyism.' Better still, dandyism was a 'suicides' club,' and the life of each of its members was simply the carrying out of a permanent suicide.

To what extent did Baudelaire realize this tension of spirit? To what extent did he merely dream of it? It is difficult to decide. Not that we need doubt his constant efforts to dress with strict elegance in order to appear perfectly dressed 'at every hour of the day and night.'

Besides, his ablutions, which *purified, cooled* and *rejuvenated,* must have had a very deep symbolic value for him. The well-washed man shines like a mineral in the sun; the water which trickles over his body washes away the memory of past faults, kills the parasitic forms of life which cling to his skin. But I am thinking rather of an element of subtle and continual falseness in his efforts. In principle, the dandy, who was a sportsman and a warrior, ought to dress and behave in a virile manner with an aristocratic austerity. 'The perfection of dress consists (in the dandy's eyes) in absolute simplicity.' [67]

But in this case what was the meaning of that dyed hair, those women's finger nails, the pink gloves and long curls—all things which the true dandy, whether Brummel or Orsay, would have stigmatized as bad taste? There was in Baudelaire a scarcely perceptible passage from the virility of dandyism to a sort of feminine coquettishness, to a feminine taste for clothes. Look at this snapshot we have of him which is truer and more alive than a portrait:

'Slowly, with a slightly swaying, slightly feminine gait, Baudelaire crossed the avenue of trees at the Porte de Namur. He was meticulously careful to avoid the mud and, if it was raining, hopped on the pointed toes of his pumps in which he liked to look at his reflection. He was freshly shaved with his hair combed back in a bunch behind his ears. He wore a soft shirt collar of snowy white which could

[67] *ibid.,* p. 59.

147

be seen above the collar of his cloak and made him look like a clergyman or an actor.' [68]

We can see that it suggests the pederast rather than the dandy. It was because dandyism was also a defense against the others. With a few of the elect, whom he knew well, Baudelaire could play this perverse game of Good and Evil. He knew to what extent he could lend himself to their judgment, flirt with their contempt; and he knew that it was possible for him to make his escape at any moment with a flap of the wings, and far above the image which he left behind in their hands become once again a freedom which eluded every judgment. It was because he had got to know their principles and their habits. He might hate or fear them, but in any case he felt at home with them. But who were the *others,* the anonymous crowd of others? He was in no way familiar with them. They were potential judges, but he did not know the rules on which their judgments were founded. The 'tyranny of the human face' would be much less frightening if there were not planted in each of the faces two eyes spying on you. There were eyes everywhere and behind the eyes consciousnesses. All these consciousnesses saw him, seized on him and silently took him in; that is to say, he remained in the bottom of their hearts, classified, packed up with a label attached to him which he hadn't seen. Was that man, who had just passed, or who had let his eyes wander over him with an expression of indifference, perhaps unaware of his famous 'difference'? Did he perhaps only see in him a bourgeois

[68] Camille Lemonnier. Quoted by E. Crépet, op. cit., p. 166.

who looked like any other bourgeois? And since his difference had to be recognized by others in order to have an objective existence, the indifferent loafer helped by a simple glance to destroy it. Supposing, on the contrary, this other regarded him as a monster. How could he fortify himself in advance against his judgment? How could he assert that he had escaped it unless he knew the reasons behind it? That was true prostitution—you belonged to everybody. The popular saying which gives the cat the right to look at a king might have terrible consequences precisely because for the cat there is no such thing as a king. 'At a show or ball,' he wrote, 'each of us enjoys everybody.' Therefore the least urchin could enjoy Baudelaire. He was naked and defenseless under his gaze. Thus by one of those contradictions to which we have grown accustomed, Baudelaire, the man of crowds, was also the man who had the greatest fear of crowds. The pleasure which he did find in the spectacle of a great throng of people was merely the pleasure of *looking*. And the person who looks, as we all know from experience, forgets that people may look at him. This disappearance of the self, of which Baudelaire has spoken in this connection, has nothing to do with pantheistic dilution. He did not lose himself in the crowd; but by observing without thinking that he himself was observed, he became in face of the mottled, moving object, a freedom which was purely contemplative. For the loafer, indeed, the sight of a street is agreeable because the passers-by are busy, wrapped up in their own affairs, absorbed by their own work and pay no attention to him. But when one of the passers-by suddenly looks up, the

149

observer finds that he is observed, the hunter that he is hunted. Baudelaire had a horror of feeling that he was a quarry. It was torture for him to go into a café, into a public place, because in this case the looks of everyone there converged on the person who had just come in; while the new arrival, taken aback and not accustomed to the place, could not defend himself by staring back at the people who were staring at him. Baudelaire developed a mania for having someone with him wherever he went, not merely, as Asselineau imagined, because 'as a poet and a dramatist he was obsessed with the idea that he must always have a public,' but chiefly so that he would always be under the gaze of someone whom he knew, under an eye that had behind it a harmless consciousness which would protect him against alien consciousnesses. In a word he was horribly shy, and we remember his misfortunes as a lecturer. He stumbled as he read, spoke so fast that he became unintelligible, kept his eyes glued to his notes and seemed to be in the worst throes of suffering. His dandyism was a defense against his shyness. His meticulous cleanliness and the neatness of his dress were the effect of constant vigilance and represented a refusal ever to be caught in the wrong. He wanted to appear impeccable to every eye; and his physical impeccability symbolized moral irreproachability. Just as the masochist only submits to humiliation by decree, so Baudelaire would not be judged without his own prior consent, that is to say, without taking precautions to elude judgment if he chose. But by a contrary movement, the oddity of his clothes and his hats, which attracted attention, was a definite assertion of his uniqueness. He wanted to cause astonishment in order to disconcert the observer. The aggressiveness of his dress was almost an act; his challenge was almost a look of bravado. The scoffer who looked at him felt that he himself had been *foreseen* and that this extravagance was *aimed at* him. If he was scandalized it was because he discovered, so to speak, a penetrating thought on the folds of the material which turned towards him and shouted: 'I *knew* you'd laugh.' He became indignant and was already less of an 'observer' and rather more 'observed.' At any rate, he was flabbergasted in just the way that Baudelaire wanted. He fell into a trap. The free and unpredictable consciousness, which might have turned Baudelaire inside out, discovered his secrets and formed the most misleading opinion of him, was, as it were, led by the hand and made to feel amused by the color of a coat or the cut of a pair of trousers. All this time the defenseless body of the *real* Baudelaire was protected. The poet's mythomania was the result of exactly the same attitude of mind. It drew a picture of a strange, scandalous Baudelaire on whom all these chattering witnesses would fasten. He was a pederast, an informer, an eater of children and heaven knew what besides; but while gossip tore the fictitious character to pieces, the other remained hidden from them. We come once again on the twofold aspect of self-punishment. For it was with a profound sense of guilt that Baudelaire was a dandy. In the first place, by getting himself condemned on faked evidence he acquired the right to despise his judges and hence to contest their best-founded judgments. But in addition, the blame which he incurred for his extrava-

151

gances, for the crimes which he imputed to himself, was a punishment which went right home though in a fictitious manner. He enjoyed the very unreality of the punishment. It stood for the symbolic satisfaction—a satisfaction which was free from danger—of his taste for chastisement and helped to diminish his feeling of guilt. With close friends Baudelaire accused himself of real failings because he knew that he could escape blame for them; with strangers, whose reactions he couldn't foresee, he accused himself of imaginary failings and escaped condemnation because he knew that he wasn't guilty of the things for which he was blamed. His dress was for the eye what his lies were for the ear—a resounding sin, a sin trumpeted from the housetops which enveloped and hid him. At the same time, he leant over this image that he had just created in the consciousness of others and the image fascinated him. After all, this perverse and eccentric dandy was *he*. The mere fact of feeling that he was the target of all those eyes created, as it were, a solidarity between himself and his lies. He saw himself; he read his own character in the eyes of others, and he enjoyed this imaginary portrait in a mood of unreality. Thus the remedy was worse than the evil. Because he was afraid of being seen, Baudelaire forced himself on people's attention. It has seemed a matter of surprise that he sometimes looked like a woman and certain writers have tried to discover in him signs of a homosexuality of which he never showed any trace. But we must remember that 'femineity' comes from a person's condition, not from his sex. The essential characteristic of woman—of the bourgeois woman—is that she depends very largely on *opinion*. She is idle and kept. She asserts herself by *pleasing;* she dresses in order to please; clothes and make-up serve partly to reveal and partly to conceal her. Any man who happened to find himself in a similar condition would probably assume an appearance of 'femineity.' This was Baudelaire's position. He did not earn his living by working which meant that the money on which he lived was not remuneration for some social service which could be appreciated objectively, but depended essentially on people's judgments of him. Yet his initial choice of himself implied an extraordinary, a constant concern for opinion. He knew that he was seen; he knew that peoples' eyes were continually on him; he wanted to please and displease at the same time. His least gesture was 'for the public.' His pride was hurt by it, but his masochism rejoiced in it. When he went out dressed up to the eyes, it was a regular ceremony. He had to look after his clothes, hop over puddles, preserve all those defensive gestures, which were a little ridiculous, by investing them with a certain grace. And the gaze which enveloped him was there. While he was going gravely through the thousand impotent little gestures which belonged to his priestly office, he felt that he was penetrated, *possessed* by other people. It was not by his bearing and his strength, not by the external signs of a social function that he tried to defend himself, to assert himself; it was by his dress and by the grace of his movements. How could he not have been woman and priest at the same time—*woman like the priest?* Did he not feel more deeply than others and in himself this connection between the priesthood and 'femineity' since he wrote in *Fusées:*

'On the femineity of the Church as a reason for her all-powerfulness'? But a man-woman is not necessarily a homosexual. The passiveness of an object under people's gaze, for which he tried to compensate by the studied artistry of his movements and his clothes, was sometimes a source of enjoyment to him; and he may, perhaps, from time to time in his dreams have transformed it into another sort of passiveness—the passiveness of his own body beneath the desire of the male. That was probably the source of the perpetual lying accusation of pederasty which he brought against himself. But if he dreamt that he was had by force, it was to satisfy his perversity and that masochism whose causes are known to us. The myth of dandyism concealed not homosexuality, but exhibitionism.

For Baudelaire's dandyism with its ferocious, sterile constraints was a myth, a dream cultivated day by day, which produced a certain number of symbolic acts, but which we know was only a dream. According to his own pronouncements, in order to be a dandy it was necessary to have been brought up in luxury, to possess a considerable fortune and to live a life of idleness. But neither the education he received nor his needy idleness fulfilled these requirements. He was certainly a *déclassé* and he suffered from the knowledge that he was. He went in for bohemianism, was the son of Madame l'Ambassadrice 'who had turned out badly.' But this *real déclassement* did not correspond in any way to the symbolic rupture which the dandy accomplished. Baudelaire did not set himself above, but below the bourgeoisie. He was kept by it in the same way that the eighteenth-century writer was kept by the nobility. His dandyism was a form of wish-fulfilment. His pride was so hurt by his humiliating circumstances, that he set to work to live his *déclassement* as though it had a different meaning—as though it were a voluntary separation. But at bottom he was not deceived; and, when he observed that Guys had too much passion to be a dandy, he knew perfectly well that the same consideration could be applied to himself. He was a poet. The giant's wings, which prevented him from walking, were the wings of the poet; the evil fortune which hung over him was the evil fortune of the poet. His dandyism was a sterile wish for something beyond poetry.

It remains true that his coquetry was both a defense against other people and the instrument of his relations with himself. In his own eyes Baudelaire did not exist sufficiently. When he looked at himself in the glass, his face was too familiar for him to be able to see it; the succession of his thoughts was too close to him for him to be able to judge them. He was hemmed in by himself and yet he could not possess himself. His chief effort was therefore directed towards *recovery*. The image of himself which he sought in the eyes of others was constantly eluding him; but it might, perhaps, be possible to see himself as others saw him. It would be sufficient to establish a distance, however small, between his eyes and his image, between his reflective lucidity and his reflected consciousness. The Narcissist who wants to desire *himself* makes up and disguises himself; then he plants himself in front of a glass in his apparel and half manages to work up a feeble desire which is directed to-

155

wards his deceptive appearance of otherness. So Baudelaire made himself up, travestied himself in order to take himself by surprise. He admits in *la Fanfarlo* that he looked at himself in every mirror; he did so because he wanted to see himself in them as he *was*. But his concern for his turn-out would reconcile his desire to discover himself from outside as a thing with his hatred of the *given*. For what he looked for in the glass was himself as he had *composed* himself. The being whose reflection he saw was not an object which was purely passive and a stranger to him because he had dressed it and made it up with his own hands; it was the image of his own activity. Thus Baudelaire tried once again to remove the contradiction between his choice of *existence* and his choice of *being*. The character whom the glasses reflected was his *existence* in the process of *being*, his *being* in the process of *existing*. And during the time that he was actually reflected in the glass he worked on his feelings and thoughts in the same way. He dressed them, made them up so that they would appear like strangers to him while remaining his own, while belonging still more closely to him because he had made them. He refused to tolerate any sort of spontaneity in himself. His lucidity at once transfixed it and he began to *act* the emotion he was about to feel. In this way he was certain of being his own master: creation came from him, but at the same time he was the object created. That is what Baudelaire meant when he spoke of his *actor's* temperament:

'When I was a child, I sometimes wanted to be pope, but a military pope, and sometimes an actor.

'The enjoyment I extracted from these two hallucinations.'

And he admits in *la Fanfarlo:*

'A thoroughly upright man from birth and a bit of a rip by way of distraction—an actor by temperament—he performed for his own enjoyment and in secret session some incomparable tragedies or, to be more accurate, tragi-comedies. If he felt himself touched or tickled by gaiety he had to take good note of it, and our hero practised roaring with laughter. If some memory brought a tear into the corner of his eye, he went across to the glass and watched himself weep. If a prostitute scratched him with a pin or a penknife in an outburst of brutal, puerile jealousy, Samuel inwardly gloried in the wound, and when he owed some twenty thousand wretched francs, he shouted joyfully:

' "What a sad, what a lamentable fate for a man of genius to be harassed by a million francs' worth of debts." ' [69]

Baudelaire's favorite occupation was travesty. He travestied his body, his feelings and his life. He pursued the impossible ideal of self-creation. He only worked in order not to owe himself to anyone but himself. He wanted to take himself up, to correct himself as one corrects a picture or a poem. He wanted to be his own poem to himself, and that was the game he played on himself. No one had had a profounder experience of

[69] *Les Paradis artificiels,* pp. 239–40.

the insoluble contradiction inherent in creative activity. Is not the aim of the creator, indeed, to produce his creation as though it were an emanation, as though it were flesh of his flesh, and does he not wish at the same time for this part of himself to stand in front of him like an alien thing? Did not Baudelaire wish to be a creator in the most radical sense because it was his own existence that he was trying to create? Yet on the sly he imposed certain limits on this very effort. When Rimbaud attempted in his turn to become the author of himself and defined his attempt by his famous 'I is another,' he did not hesitate to bring about a radical transformation of his thought. He undertook the systematic derangement of all his senses; he smashed this pretended nature which was derived from his bourgeois birth and which was only a habit. He was not putting on an act; he really did set out to produce extraordinary thoughts and feelings. Baudelaire, on the other hand, stopped half-way. When faced with that total solitude where living and invention were identical, where his reflective lucidity was diluted into his reflected spontaneity, he became afraid. Rimbaud didn't waste his time working up a horror of nature; he simply smashed it like a money-box. Baudelaire smashed nothing at all. His work as a creator merely consisted in the travestying and the ordering of things. He accepted all the suggestions which came from his spontaneous consciousness. He simply wanted to touch them up a little, forcing them here, toning them down there. He was not going to indulge in roars of laughter when he felt like crying. He would weep 'more truly than nature.' That was all. The conclusion of his act would be the poem which would offer him the image —re-thought, recreated and objectified—of the emotion which he had half felt. Baudelaire was a pure creator of form; Rimbaud created form and matter.

These precautions turned out to be quite inadequate. Baudelaire at once became afraid of his own autonomy. The aim of dandyism, the cult of artificiality and his act was to put him in possession of himself. Suddenly, he was seized with a feeling of anguish; and he abdicated. He no longer wanted anything except to be an inanimate object whose works were external. Sometimes it was to his physiological heredity that he appealed to relieve him of his freedom:

> 'I'm ill, ill. I've got an execrable temperament through the fault of my parents. Because of them I'm falling to pieces. That's what comes of being the child of a mother of twenty-seven and a father of seventy-two. A disproportionate, pathological, senile union. Think of it—forty-five years' difference between them. You tell me that you're doing physiology under Claude Bernard. Well, ask your master what he thinks of the chancy fruit of such a coupling.'

It will be seen that there is a mixture of passion and caution here. His resignation, his complete surrender to the body and to heredity must be sanctioned by a judge. But to ensure that the verdict shall be more crushing, he adds ten years on to his father's age. In this way, he will be able, if he feels disposed, to escape from the physiological malediction. The sentence of the expert will be

159

terrible; it will be just enough to make him feel the fear that he wants to feel; but his fear will not be quite real because his trial is based on evidence which he himself has falsified. We come once more upon the mechanism which we described above. Baudelaire always left himself a loophole.

On other occasions he resorted to the Devil. He wrote to Flaubert in 1860:

> 'All my life I've been obsessed by the impossibility of finding an explanation of certain of man's sudden actions or thoughts without the hypothesis of the intervention of an evil force which is external to him.' [70]

And in the *Petits poèmes en prose:*

> 'I have more than once been the victim of those crises and those *élans* which are grounds for thinking that malicious demons slip inside us and make us carry out their absurdest wishes without our being aware of it . . . the spirit of mystification . . . plays a large part . . . in this mood—doctors describe it as hysterical and those who are a little more orthodox than the doctors call it satanic—which drives us without any resistance on our part into a host of actions which are dangerous or unseemly.' [71]

Mystification and gratuitous acts, which were two of the essential rites of dandyism, suddenly becomes the result of diabolical and external impulses. Baudelaire

[70] *Lettres,* 1841–1866, pp. 267–8.   [71] 'Le Mauvais vitrier,' p. 23.

is no more than a marionette whose strings are being manipulated. It is repose—the great repose of stone and inanimate beings. At bottom it matters little whether he attributes his actions to the Devil or to Hysteria; the essential is that he is not their cause, but their victim. After that, we notice that he has, as usual, left the door open. He doesn't believe in the Devil.

In short, he spared no pains to transform his life in his own eyes into a destiny. That only happens, as Malraux has well shown, at the moment of death. And, said Greek wisdom, which of us can say that he is happy or unhappy until he's dead? A gesture, a breath, a thought may suddenly alter the sense of the whole of the past—such is man's temporal condition. Baudelaire had a horror of this responsibility which suddenly laid on his shoulders the burden of the whole of his past. He did not want to be subject to the iron law by which our present behavior is continually modifying our past acts. In order for the past to be what it is—irremediable and incapable of perfection—and for the present itself to be able to barter its verdure and its disquieting disponibility against the immutability of the bygone years, he chose to consider his life from the point of view of death as though it had been suddenly frozen by a premature end. He pretended to have killed himself; and, if he often laughed at the idea of suicide, it was also because it allowed him at any moment to imagine that he had just put a stop to his life. At every moment, though still alive, he was already on the other side of the grave. He had performed the operation of which Malraux speaks; his 'irremediable existence' was there under his eyes like a destiny. He could draw a line under it as though it were a sum and add up the total. At every moment he was in a position to sit down and write *Memoirs of My Dead Life.* Thus the proud free criminal, the Don Juan of hell, the rebel was also at the same time the *poète maudit,* the Devil's marionette, the corrupt and condemned child of a disproportionate couple. But above everything else he was the crucified victim of fate in the manner of ancient times. For once no one was looking at him. He wanted to forget that it was his own look that froze him; but underneath the novelty of his *Existence,* which was continually renewed, he perceived the features of a fixed unchangeable face which he called his *Being:*

> *Un navire pris dans le pôle*
> *Comme en un piège de cristal*
> *Cherchant par quel détroit fatal*
> *Il est tombé dans cette geôle . . .*

Thus once again he could play a double game. His sense of freedom made the knowledge that his destiny was absolutely unalterable seem every moment less intolerable to him; but the certainty that he had a destiny was a perpetual excuse for his shortcomings and the trick that he relied on to lighten the burden of his autonomy. If death is everywhere present in his work, if 'more even than life it holds [him] in its subtle thrall,' it is first and foremost because death was invoked by his intense sense of his own uniqueness. For nothing is unique except the transitory, except 'what will never be seen a second time.' But the very fact that it was bound to end made this existence appear as though it had *already* ended. If

162

it had to end, it mattered little whether the end came today or tomorrow. The end was already there in the present. And all at once everything—even the moment that he was actually living—seemed to belong to the past as it does in the illusion that comes from a false recognition. But if life in the present was spontaneous, unpredictable, inexplicable, life in the past was a life of explanations, a chain of causes and reasons. Baudelaire, who hesitated between the feeling that everything was irreparable and the feeling that everything could still begin, took precautions so that he was always in a position to jump from one to the other as it suited his interests.

For it is not enough to say that he resorted to intellectual subterfuges in order to give his life a faded appearance. He deliberately operated a radical conversion; he chose to advance backwards with his face turned towards the past, crouching on the floor of the car which was taking him away with his eyes fixed on the disappearing road. Few existences have been more stagnant than his. For him the die was already cast at the age of twenty-one. Everything had stopped. He had had his chance and lost for ever. By 1846 he had spent half his capital, written most of his poems, given his relations with his parents their definitive form, contracted the venereal disease which slowly rotted him, met the woman who would weigh like lead on every hour of his life and made the voyage which provided the whole of his work with exotic images. There had been a brief flare-up, one of those 'jolts' of which he often spoke; then the fire went out. There was nothing left for him but to become a survival. Long before he was thirty his opinions were formed and for the rest of his life he did no more than ruminate over them. One's heart bleeds when one reads *Fusées* and *Mon coeur mis à nu*. There is nothing new in these notes, which were put together towards the end of his life, nothing that he had not said a hundred times before and said better. Conversely, *la Fanfarlo,* a work written in his earliest youth, produces a feeling of stupefaction. Everything—the ideas and the form—is already there. Critics have often drawn attention to the mastery of this twenty-three-year-old writer. From that moment onwards he did nothing but repeat himself. With his mother it was always the same quarrels, the same complaints, the same promises; with his creditors always the same struggles; with Ancelle always the same squabbles over money; he always succumbed to the same weaknesses and condemned them in the same terms; and when he was in the depths of despair he was always buoyed up by the same hopes. He wrote about the work of Others, took up his old poems and revised them, became ecstatic over literary plans of which the oldest dated back to his youth. He translated the stories of Edgar Poe; but the creator created nothing more; he rehashed old work. A hundred removals and not a single voyage. He did not even possess the strength to go and live at Honfleur. Social events passed over him, leaving him untouched. True, he became a little agitated in 1848, but he did not take any real interest in the Revolution. He simply wanted to see General Aupick's house set on fire. For the rest, he soon sank back into his morose dreams of social stagnation. He fell to pieces rather than evolved.

164

Year after year we find him just the same, simply older, gloomier, his mind less rich and less alert, his body more battered. And for those who have followed him step by step the final dementia appears less like an accident than the logical outcome of his downfall.

This long and painful dissolution was chosen. Baudelaire chose to live his life backwards. He lived in a period which had just invented the future. Jean Cassou has described the immense current of ideas and hopes which carried the French towards the future.[72] After the seventeenth century which rediscovered the past and the eighteenth century which made an inventory of the present, the nineteenth century believed that it had discovered a fresh dimension of time and the world. For the sociologists, the humanists and the manufacturers who discovered the power of capital, for the proletariat which was becoming conscious of itself, for Marx and for Flora Tristan, for Michelet, for Proudhon and for George Sand, the future existed and gave the present its meaning. The present phase was transitory and could only really be understood in relation to an era of social justice for which it was preparing the way. It is difficult today to realize the power of this great revolutionary and reformist current. We therefore fail to appreciate the power that Baudelaire had to exert to swim against the tide. If he had given up the struggle he would have been carried away, forced to declare his belief in the Becoming of humanity and to celebrate Progress. It was the last thing that he wanted to do. He hated Progress because Progress made the future state of a system the cause and

[72] '1848' in *Anatomie des Révolutions* (N.R.F.).

165

explanation of its present state. Progress meant the primacy of the future and the future justified long-term undertakings. Baudelaire, who did not *want* to undertake anything, turned his back on the future. When he thought of the future of humanity, it was in the form of a fatal dissolution:

'The world is coming to an end. The only reason why it might last is that it exists. How feeble this reason is compared with all those which proclaim the contrary, particularly this one: What is there left under the sun for the world to do?'[73]

In other places he dreams of the destruction of 'our Western races.' As for his personal future, if he sometimes thought of it, it was in terms of a catastrophe:

'I'm not positively old,' he wrote in December 1855, 'but I may soon become old.'[74]

In 1859 he returned to the charge:

'Supposing I were to become infirm or feel that my brain was going before I had done everything which it seems to me that I must and can do.'[75]

In still another place:

'There is something more serious . . . than physical suffering—it's the fear of seeing one's admirable poetic faculty, the clarity of one's ideas and the power of hope, which in reality are my capital, become used

[73] *Fusées.*   [74] *Corres. gén.,* 1, p. 351.   [75] *Corres. gén.,* 2, p. 398.

up, disintegrate and disappear in this horrible exist-
ence which is full of jolts.'[76]

For Baudelaire the principal dimension of temporality
was the past. It was the past which gave meaning to the
present; but this past was not an imperfect prefiguration
or the *prior* existence of objects which were simply equal
in power and dignity to the objects that one knew. The
relation between present and past was Progress in re-
verse. That meant that the old determined the new and
explained it in exactly the same way that for Comte the
higher explained and determined the lower. The finality
implied by the idea of Progress had not disappeared in
Baudelaire—rather the reverse—but it was inverted. In
the progressionist conception of finality, it is the future
statue which explains and determines the cast on which
the sculptor is at present working. For Baudelaire the
statue was lodged in the past and it was from its place
in the past that it explained to its present ruins the crude
piracy which aimed at reproducing it. The social system
which he favoured was such in its strict and perfect
hierarchy that it would not countenance any attempt at
improvement. If there were any alteration it was because
it had begun to decay. It was the same with the indi-
vidual. Duration could only lead to senility and decom-
position. It was, I think, Gelhart who, speaking of the
Romans in the fifth century, described them as wander-
ing about in a town which was too big for them and
which was full of departed splendor, of wonderful
and mysterious monuments which they could neither

[76] *Corres. gén.,* I, p. 353.

understand nor remake and which seemed to them to be evidence of the existence of ancestors who had been wiser and abler than they. That is more or less the sort of world in which Baudelaire chose to live. He took care to see that his present was haunted by a past which crushed it. What is more, it was not a question—this was the essential difference between his feeling and the sense of Progress—of a continuous decline which was such that every moment was inferior to the one that preceded it. What counted was that an exquisite, peerless form had once appeared in the far-off mists of life or of history and that all individual enterprises and all social institutions were simply guilty or unworthy copies of it. Baudelaire suffered deeply from the success of the idea of Progress because his age snatched him away from the contemplation of the past and compelled him to turn his eyes towards the future. In this way he was made to live his age backwards; and in such a situation he felt as clumsy and embarrassed as a man who was being made to walk backwards. He found no rest until from 1852 onwards Progress became in its turn an empty dream of the Past. In the dreary, pedestrian society of the Empire which was overcome by the anxiety to maintain and restore, which was haunted by memories of glory and great vanished hopes, he was able to lead his stagnant life in peace, able to continue his slow stumbling walk backwards at his ease. We must examine more closely this extreme cult of the past. We have seen that it originally represented a certain effort to escape from freedom: character and destiny were great gloomy appearances which only revealed themselves in the past.

168

The man who thought of himself as 'irritable' limited himself at bottom to observing that he had often been irritated. Baudelaire turned to the past in order to limit freedom by character. But his choice had other meanings. He had a horror of feeling that time was running out. It seemed to him that it was his own blood which was running out. The time which passed was *lost* time, the time of laziness and listlessness, the time of the thousand promises that you made yourself and hadn't kept, the time of removals, commissions and the perpetual hunt for money. But it was also the time of *ennui,* the eruption of the Present which was always beginning anew. And the present was identical with Baudelaire's stale and tenacious awareness of himself, with the translucid limbo of his inner life:

'I assure you that the seconds are now strongly and solemnly accentuated and that each one which comes echoing out of the clock says: "I am life, intolerable, implacable life." ' [77]

In a sense what Baudelaire fled from into the Past was enterprises, plans and perpetual instability. Like the schizophrenic and the melancholic, he justified his incapacity for action by turning towards what was *already lived, already done,* what was past recall. But in a different sense he sought above everything else to free himself from himself. His reflective lucidity showed him that he existed on a short-term basis like a succession of pale desires and affections which were paralysed by the void,

[77] *Petits poèmes en prose,* 'La Chambre Double,' p. 14.

that he knew himself through and through, and that nevertheless he had to go on living, as it were, drop by drop. In order to see himself not as he had made himself, but as Other People, as God saw him, as he *was,* he would have had in the end to seize his own Nature. And this Nature belonged to the past. What I am is what I was because my present freedom always casts a doubt on the nature that I have acquired. At the same time, Baudelaire had not chosen to renounce this lucid consciousness which was the source of his dignity and his uniqueness. His dearest wish was to *be* like the stone and the statue enjoying the peaceful repose which belonged to the unchangeable; but he wanted this calm impenetrability, this permanence, this total adhesion of the self to the self to be conferred on his free consciousness in so far as it was free and was consciousness. Now the Past offered him the image of this impossible synthesis of being and existence. My past is I, but this I is definitive. What I did six years, ten years ago, was done once and for all. Nothing can prevent my consciousness of my faults, of my virtues, of my affections from standing, massive and irremediable, on my horizon like the mile-stone which the car that is taking me away has already passed and which contracts indefinitely and fades into the distance under my eyes. What *is,* indeed, is that I *have had* this consciousness: I have been hungry, I have been irritated, I have suffered, I have rejoiced. In each case, the core of my feeling lay in the consciousness that I had of it. And this hesitant consciousness, which was so unsure of itself, was saddled with the infinite responsibility for itself. It was because I was conscious of them that hunger and pleasure existed. At present I am no longer responsible for them or, at any rate, not in the same manner. This consciousness is over there like a stone in my path. And yet it remains consciousness. And, no doubt, these petrified consciousnesses do not really belong to me; they are not inherent in me as my present consciousness is inherent in itself. But Baudelaire chose to *be* this conscious Past. What he overlooked, what he took for a lesser being was his actual feeling. He devalued it with the intention of making it less urgent, less present. He turned the present into a past whose importance had been diminished so that he could deny its reality. In that respect he resembles to some extent a writer like Faulkner who has turned away from the future in the same way and become someone who despises the present in the interest of the past. But for Faulkner the past can be seen through the present like a diamond block through a surface disorder: he makes a frontal attack on the reality of the present. Baudelaire was abler and craftier. He never dreamed of explicitly denying this reality; he simply refused to admit that it possessed any value. Value belongs to the past alone because the past *is;* and if the present offers a certain appearance of beauty or goodness, it is because it borrows it from the past as the moon borrows its light from the sun. The *moral* dependence of the present stands symbolically for a dependence of being because the finished form must in sound logic precede its degradations. In a word, he asked the past to be the eternity which changed him into himself. There was in Baudelaire a radical confusion between the past and eternity.

171

Is not the past definitive, unchangeable, out of reach? Thus Baudelaire came to know the bitter pleasures of decadence and communicated a taste for it like a virus to his Symbolist disciples. To live means to fall; the present is a fall. It was by remorse and regret that Baudelaire chose to feel his links with the past. It was a vague remorse which was sometimes intolerable and sometimes delicious and which at bottom was nothing but the mode of apprehending his memories in concrete form. By his memories he asserted his profound solidarity with the man that he had been; and, at the same time, he managed to safeguard his freedom. He was free because he was guilty and because for him a fault was the commonest manifestation of freedom. He turns towards this past which he *is* and which he imagines that he has smirched. He managed to appropriate at a distance his own essence and in doing so he recovers his perverse pleasure in wrongdoing. But this time he was not preaching against virtue as it was taught; he was preaching against himself. And the more involved he became with evil, the more opportunities he had for repenting; the more alive, the more pressing his memories of what he had been became, the more solid and the more apparent became the link which united him to his essence.

But we must go farther than this and discover in this relationship with the past the essential of what we shall call Baudelaire's *poetic reality*. Every poet pursues in his own way this synthesis of existence and being which, as we have already seen, is an impossibility. Their quest leads them to choose certain objects in the world which seem to them to be the most eloquent symbols of that reality in which existence and being would merge, and to try to appropriate them to themselves through contemplation. Appropriation, as we have shown in another place, is an attempt at identification. Thus they are led to create by means of signs certain ambiguous natures, a shimmer of existence and being which is doubly satisfying, because these natures are at once objective essences which the poets may contemplate and because they proceed from the poets who may find themselves again in them. The object which Baudelaire created in his poems by a perpetual emanation and, equally, by the actions of his life is what he called, and what we will call after him, the *spiritual*. The spiritual was Baudelaire's poetic reality. The spiritual was a *being* and revealed itself as such; it possessed the objectivity, the permanence and the identity which belong to being. But inside this being there was something which resembled restraint; we cannot say that it *is* completely; a profound discretion prevents it not from revealing itself, but from asserting itself in the manner of a table or a pebble. It is characterized by a sort of absence; it is never completely there or completely visible. It remains suspended between the void and being by a discretion which is pushed to the extreme limit. We can enjoy it; it does not hide itself; but this contemplative enjoyment has, so to speak, a secret levity: it enjoys not being able to enjoy enough. It is self-evident that this metaphysical levity of Baudelaire's world represents *existence* itself. Anyone who has read the admirable lines from *le Guignon:*

173

Mainte fleur épanche à regret
Son parfum doux comme un secret
Dans les solitudes profondes

—will have perceived Baudelaire's taste for those strange objects which resemble the outcroppings of being and whose spirituality consists of absence. The perfume exists *à regret,* and we breathe this 'regret' in with it; it makes its escape at the same time that it gives itself; it enters our nostrils and vanishes, melts away on the spot. But not quite; it is there and brushes clingingly against us. It is for this reason—and not, as frivolous people have claimed, because his sense of smell was highly developed—that Baudelaire was so fond of scents. The smell of a body is the body itself which we breathe in with our nose and mouth, which we suddenly possess as though it were its most secret substance and, to put the matter in a nutshell, its nature. The smell which is in me is the fusion of the body of the other person with my body; but it is the other person's body with the flesh removed, a vaporized body which has remained completely itself but which has become a volatile spirit. Baudelaire was particularly fond of this spiritualized possession. We often have the impression that he 'smelt' women rather than made love to them; but in addition to this perfumes had a special power for him. While giving themselves unreservedly they evoked an inaccessible beyond. They were at once bodies and, as it were, the negation of the body. There was in them something unsatisfied which merged into Baudelaire's perpetual desire to be somewhere else:

Comme d'autres esprits voguent sur la musique
Le mien, ô mon amour! nage sur ton parfum.

For the same reasons he preferred dusk, the blurred skies of Holland, the *jours blancs tièdes et voilés,* the *jeunes corps maladifs*—all the beings, things and people which seemed wounded, broken or slipping towards their end; the *petites vieilles* as well as the light of a lamp which grew pale as day broke and seemed to flicker in its being. The lovely women, too, whom we meet in his poems seek to evoke by their indolence and their dumbness an inexpressible reticence. Moreover, they are adolescents; they are not yet in full bloom, and the lines which describe them possess the art of suggesting that they are nonchalant young animals which glide over the surface of the earth without leaving a trace, which glide over the surface of life—absent, bored, cold and smiling, and completely absorbed in futile ceremonies. Like Baudelaire, therefore, we will describe as *spiritual* the thing which allows itself to be apprehended by the senses and which most resembles consciousness. The whole of Baudelaire's efforts were devoted to the recovery of his consciousness, to possessing it like an object in the hollow of his hand. That is why he caught in full flight everything which bore any resemblance to an objectified consciousness—perfumes, subdued lights, distant music were so many tiny, mute, given consciousnesses, so many images of his unseizable existence which were at once absorbed and consumed like hosts. He was haunted by the desire to touch and feel thoughts which had become objects—his own incarnate thoughts:

'I have always thought that foul and revolting animals were, perhaps, only the vivification, the corporealization, the flowering in material form of man's *evil thoughts*.'[78]

His poems themselves are 'corporealized' thoughts not simply because they have assumed bodily form in the signs employed, but mainly because each of them by its skilful rhythm, the deliberately hesitating and almost vanished sense which it gives to words and also because by an ineffable grace it is a restrained, fleeting existence exactly like a scent.

But what comes nearest to a woman's perfume is the *meaning of a thing*. An object which has a meaning points over its shoulder to another object, a general situation, hell or heaven. The meaning, which is an image of human transcendence, is like an unfulfilled transcendence of the object by itself. It exists under our eyes, but it is not really visible: it is a furrow in the air, a motionless direction. Meaning is an intermediary between the present thing which supports it and the absent object which it designates; it retains within itself a little of the former and already points to the latter. It is never completely pure; there is in it, as it were, the memory of the forms and colors from which it emanates; and yet it gives itself like a being beyond being. It does not exhibit itself; it holds itself back, vacillates a little and is only accessible to the keenest senses. For Baudelaire whose spleen always demanded an 'elsewhere,' it was the

[78] Letter to Alphonse Toussenel of January 21st, 1856. (*Corres. gén.*, I, p. 370.)

very symbol of non-satisfaction; a thing which has meaning is always an unsatisfied thing. Its meaning is the image of thought, and it gives itself like an *existence* swallowed up in *being*. It will be seen that in Baudelaire the words 'perfume,' 'thought' and 'secret' are more or less synonymous:

> *Parfois on trouve un vieux flacon qui se souvient*
> *D'où jaillit toute vive une âme qui revient.*
> *Mille pensers dormaient, chrysalides funèbres,*
> *Frémissant doucement dans les lourdes ténèbres*
> *Qui dégagent leurs ailes et prennent leur essor . . .*[79]
>
> *   *   *
>
> *Armoire à doux secrets, pleine de bonnes choses,*
>   *De vins, de parfums . . .*[80]
>
> *   *   *
>
> *Mainte fleur épanche à regret*
> *Son parfum doux comme un secret.*[81]

If Baudelaire was so fond of 'secrets,' it was because they were the manifestation of a perpetual *Beyond*. The man who has a secret is not entirely contained in his body or in the present moment. He is elsewhere; we can feel it in his unsatisfied, absent-minded expression. Lightened by his secret, he weighs less heavily on the present; his *being* is less oppressive or, as Heidegger puts it, for his friends and his fellows he does not reduce himself to what he is. Yet the secret is an objective being which can be revealed by signs or which a dumb-show may enable us to divine. In a certain sense it is right

[79] *Fleurs du mal:* 'Le Flacon.'   [80] *ibid.,* 'Le Beau Navire.'
[81] *ibid.,* 'Le Guignon.'

outside in front of us who are its witnesses; but it scarcely lets itself be divined; it is suggested, evoked by the expression of the face, by an attitude, by a few ambiguous words. Thus this being, which is the underlying nature of the thing, is also its subtlest essence. It scarcely *is;* and all meaning, in so far as its discovery is arduous, may be regarded as a secret. That is why Baudelaire hunted passionately for the perfumes and the secrets of everything. That is why he tried to wrench their meaning even from colors; that is why he wrote of violet color that it stands for:

'Love which is repressed, mysterious, veiled, the color of a deaconess.' [82]

If he borrowed the rather vague idea of 'correspondences' from Swedenborg, it was not so much because he adhered to the metaphysical system which it implied; it was rather because he wanted to find in each reality a fixed non-satisfaction, an appeal to another thing, an objectified transcendence. It was because he wanted to 'pass through a forest of symbols which observed him with familiar looks.' Ultimately, these acts of transcendence would extend to the whole world. The world as totality would have meaning and in this hierarchical order of objects which consented to lose themselves in order to indicate other objects, Baudelaire would find once more his own image. The purely material universe was as far removed from him as possible; but in the universe which was invested with meaning Baudelaire

[82] *Fusées.*

178

would recover. Has he not written in *l'Invitation au voyage* in the *Petits poèmes en prose:*

> 'In such a calm lovely country as this . . . wouldn't you be framed in your analogy and wouldn't you be reflected, to talk like the mystics, in your own correspondence?'

Such was the term of Baudelaire's efforts—to take possession of himself in his eternal 'difference,' to realize his Otherness by identifying himself with the whole World. Lightened, hollowed out, filled with signs and symbols, this world which enfolded him in its immense totality was nothing but himself; and he was himself the Narcissus who wanted to embrace and contemplate himself. Beauty itself was not a sensual perfection contained within the narrow limits of a frame, a poetic *genre,* a musical air. First and foremost it was suggestion, that is to say, it was this strange, forged type of reality where being and existence merged, where existence was objectified and solidified by being, where being was lightened by existence. If he admired Constantin Guys, it was because he saw in him 'the painter of circumstance and of all that it suggested of eternity.'
In another place he wrote:

> 'It is this admirable, this immortal sense of Beauty which makes us regard the Earth and its sights as a glimpse, a *correspondence* of Heaven. Our insatiable thirst for everything which is beyond and which is revealed by life is the most living proof of our immortality. It is at once by and *through* poetry, by

and *through* music that the soul catches a glimpse of the splendors which lie on the other side of the grave; and when an exquisite poem brings tears to our eyes, these tears are not the proof of excessive enjoyment; they are much more the sign of an irritated melancholy, a nervous postulation, a nature exiled in an imperfect world which would like to take possession at once on this very earth of a revealed paradise. Thus the principle of poetry is strictly and simply human aspiration towards a higher beauty and this principle appears in an enthusiasm, an elevation of soul; an enthusiasm which is completely independent of passion, which is the intoxication of the heart, and of truth which is the field of reason. For passion is a *natural* thing, too natural, indeed, not to introduce a painful, discordant note into the realm of pure beauty; too familiar not to scandalize the pure Desires, the gracious Melancholy, the noble Despair which dwell in the supernatural regions of poetry.' [83]

The whole of Baudelaire is in this passage. We meet once again his horror of a nature which is too opulent, his taste for being unsatisfied and for pleasures which irritate the senses, his aspiration towards the beyond. But let us make no mistake about this last aspiration. People have spoken of Baudelaire's Platonism or of his mysticism as though he wished to put off the bonds of the flesh and to find himself, in the manner of the Philosopher described in *The Banquet*, face to face with pure

[83] *l'Art romantique*, pp. 159–60.

180

Ideas or absolute beauty. In fact, we do not find in his work the slightest trace of this effort which belongs to the Mystics and which is accompanied by a complete renunciation of earthly things, by a shedding of individuality. If nostalgia for the beyond, non-satisfaction and an attempt to transcend the real are everywhere present in his work, it was at the very heart of this reality that he poured out his lamentations. In his work, the attempt to transcend showed itself, began with the things which surrounded him. It was absolutely essential that they should be there so that Baudelaire could have the pleasure of transcending them. He would have been horrified at the idea of ascending into heaven and leaving the treasures of the earth behind him. What he wanted was those same treasures, but in such a way that he could despise them. He wanted the earthly prison so that he could feel that he was continually on the point of escaping from it. In short, his non-satisfaction was not a true aspiration towards the beyond, but a particular manner of illuminating the world. For Baudelaire, as for the Epicurean, the world alone counted; but they did not adopt the same manner of coming to terms with it. In the passage which we have just quoted, the higher Beauty is sought and glimpsed *through* Poetry. It is precisely that which counts—the movement which goes through the poem like a sword, which emerges from it in the direction of the beyond, but which at that point, having fulfilled its task, vanishes into the void. At bottom it is a trick for investing things with souls. He gives the trick away in the celebrated passage in *Fusées* in which the Beautiful is defined as 'Something a little

181

vague which leaves room for conjecture.' Moreover, in Baudelaire Beauty is always *particular*. Or rather what intoxicated him was a certain dose of the individual and the eternal, in which the eternal allowed one to catch a glimpse of it behind the individual.

'The beautiful,' he said, 'is composed of an eternal, unvarying element of which the quantity is excessively difficult to determine, and of a relative, circumstantial element which is, if you like, in turn or all together, period, fashion, morality, passion.' [84]

But if we ask more precisely what can possibly be the meanings of which the loafer, the hashish eater or the poet catch a glimpse through things, we are forced to admit that they do not bear any resemblance to Platonic ideas or Aristotelian forms. No doubt Baudelaire could write:

'The enthusiasm which applies itself to anything except abstractions is a sign of weakness and sickness.'

But in fact we nowhere see him setting to work on a particular nature and trying to discover the essential abstract features which are characteristic of it. 'Essences' mattered very little to him and the Socratic dialectic was foreign to him. Obviously, what he was aiming at through this or that woman who went by, whether she was Dorothée or the Malabar woman, was not *femineity,* that is to say, the ensemble of characteristics which

[84] *l'Art romantique*, p. 52.

were distinctive of her sex; and he might have said with the Greek opponent of the Academy: 'I see the horse, but I do not see horseness.' It is sufficient to re-read the *Fleurs du mal* to understand the position: what Baudelaire asked of meaning was not that it should transcend the object signified as the universal transcends the particular on which it is founded; he asked that as a mode of being it should be lighter so that it could transcend a being which was heavier and denser, as air escapes from the porous, thinking earth and above all as the soul passes through the body:

> *Il est de forts parfums pour qui toute matière*
> *Est poreuse. On dirait qu'ils pénètrent le verre.*

This impression of the penetration of the densest solid by a gassy matter whose *spirituality* lay in its inconsistency is essential in his work. The glass which is bathed in perfume and which is at once sharp, polished, without memory, but which is haunted by a residual element, permeated by a vapor, is the clearest symbol of the relationship which existed for him between the thing which had meaning and its meaning. Now it is evident that the thing and its meaning are separate. The glassy, diaphanous quality of *meaning,* its spectral, unalterable character provide the clue: meaning is the *past.* A thing possessed meaning for Baudelaire when it was, so to speak, porous for a certain past and stimulated the mind to go beyond it in the direction of memory. Charles Du Bos has rightly said that 'For Baudelaire the only thing that was *profound* was the past. It was the past which gave to everything, imprinted on everything a third

183

dimension.'[85] Thus, just as we have pointed out the confusion between the eternal and the past, so we can now point out the confusion between the past and the spiritual. Like Bergson's, Baudelaire's work might well be called *Matière et mémoire*. It is because the universal past—and not merely the past of his consciousness—was seen to be a mode of being which was in complete conformity with his wishes. It *is* because it is unalterable and a pure object of passive contemplation; but at the same time it is *absent,* is out of reach, delicately faded; it possesses that ghostly being which Baudelaire called *spirit* and which was the only one with which the poet could come to terms. His meditations on dead pleasures were accompanied by that irritation, that postulation of the nerves and that sense of being unsatisfied which were dear to him. The past was *far away—déjà plus loin que l'Inde ou la Chine*—and yet nothing was closer. It was the being beyond being. It was the 'secret' of old women who had suffered, of those gloomy men whose 'ambitions had been darkly repressed,' and finally it was the secret of Satan, the only one among the angels who possessed a personal memory. Baudelaire admits on several occasions that for him the ideal being would be an object existing *in the present* with all the characteristics of a memory (*Souvenir*).

In *l'Art romantique* he expressed the wish that 'the past, while retaining the piquancy of a phantom, would recover the light and movement of its life and would make itself into the present.'[86]

[85] *Approximations,* 5 ème série, Paris, 1932, p. 41.
[86] P. 51.

In the *Fleurs du mal*:

Charme profond, magique, dont nous grise
Dans le présent le passé restauré.' [87]

In his eyes it would in effect be the objective union of
being and existence which, as we have seen, his poems
attempt to realize.

Such in its main outlines would be the portrait of Bau-
delaire. But the description which we have attempted
is inferior to the portrait in this respect—that it is suc-
cessive instead of being simultaneous. Alone the glimpse
of a face, of a man's behavior could make us feel that
the characteristics mentioned here, one after the other,
are in fact built into an indissoluble synthesis in which
each of them expresses itself and all the others at the
same time. It would be sufficient for us to see the living
Baudelaire, if only for a moment, for our scattered re-
marks to be transformed into total knowledge. Immedi-
ate perception, indeed, is accompanied by a confused
comprehension or, to borrow Heidegger's expression,
'pre-ontological' comprehension. It often takes years to
make this comprehension explicit and it contains the
principal characteristics of the object collected together
in a syncretic indifferentiation. In the absence of this
immediate comprehension, we can at any rate by way of
conclusion underline the close interdependence of all
Baudelaire's lines of conduct and all his affections, insist
on the way in which by a peculiar dialectic each trait
'passes' into the others or lets them be seen or appeals to

[87] XXXVIII, II.

them to complete themselves. This tension—this vain, arid and, so to speak, exasperated tension—which constituted Baudelaire's inner climate and which was apparent for those who knew him in the dry, cutting tone of his voice, the cold nervousness of his movements, was no doubt the result of his hatred of the nature which was inside and outside him. It appears as an effort to 'pull out' without loss, to go his own way. We cannot do better than compare his hatred of nature with the contemptuous, anguished, paralyzed attitude of a prisoner in a flooded cellar who, as he sees the water creeping up his body, throws his head backwards so that the noblest part of him, the seat of thought and sight, will at any rate remain above the muddy waters as long as possible. But this stoic attitude was also responsible for the division of himself into two people which Baudelaire pursued at all levels. He held himself back, put on the brake, judged himself; he was his own witness and own executioner, the knife which turns in the wound and the chisel which fashions the marble. He had a hold on himself and worked on himself so that for himself he would never be something given, so that he could assume at every moment the responsibility for what he was. In this sense it would be very difficult to distinguish the tension which he imposed on himself from his habit of becoming a laughing stock for himself. Whether it was torture or lucidity, looked at from another angle this tension appears as the essence of dandyism and as a stoic *ascesis;* and it was simultaneously a horror of life, a perpetual fear of soiling and compromising himself. The censorship which it exercised over his spontaneity was the equivalent of deliberate sterilization. By repressing all his *élans,* by perching himself with a single movement and for ever on the plane of reflection, Baudelaire chose a symbolic suicide; he killed himself gradually. This tension also produced the climate of Baudelairean 'Evil.' For with Baudelaire the crime was concerted, carried out deliberately and almost under duress. Evil did not correspond in any way to abandonment. It was a counter-Good which had to possess all the characteristics of Good except that they appeared with a different mathematical sign in front of them. And since Good stood for effort, exercise, self-domination, we shall find all these characteristics in Evil. Thus Baudelaire's 'tension' felt that it was accursed and wanted to be accursed. In the same way his taste for restrained pleasures of which we have already spoken expressed his hatred of any sort of abandonment and for that reason was identical with his frigidity, his sterility, his complete lack of charity and generosity, in short with the tension which we have just described. What he wanted to do was to find that he was in control of himself again, in the midst of his pleasures he had to feel the bit which pulled him back when he was on the point of surrendering to pleasure. In this sense, the phantasms—his judges, his mother, the cold beautiful women who observed him—which he evoked at the moment of the sexual act were destined to save him at the moment when he was about to submerge himself in pure sensation; and it would seem that even his impotence was provoked by fear or deriving *too much* pleasure from the sexual act. But, on the other hand, if he restrained himself in his pleasures, it was also because

187

he remained unsatisfied on principle, because he had *chosen* to find what he called his *volupté* in being unsatisfied rather than in possession. The end which he pursued was, as we know, that strange image of himself which was to be the indissoluble union of existence and being. Now it was out of reach and at bottom he knew it. He thought to reach it and actually touched it, but when he wanted to grasp it it vanished. In order therefore to conceal this defeat from himself he wanted to persuade himself that this furtive fingering was true appropriation and, by a generalized modification of all his desires, he sought this irritating form of contact in every sphere to prove to himself that it was the only kind of possession which was desirable. Thus he elected to confuse the satisfaction of desire with its unsatisfied exasperation. And that was also due to the fact that he never had any other end except himself. Now in sexual pleasure in its normal forms you enjoy the object and forget yourself, whereas in this maddening titillation you enjoy the desire, that is to say, yourself. And once again he conferred another meaning on this life with its false issue which he had made his own, on this nervous irritation from which there was no rest—it represented the radical non-satisfaction of the fallen god. He used it as a weapon to assuage his rancor. He showed himself to his mother in the throes of his sufferings; but if we examine these sufferings we find that they were identical with his pleasures. It is all the same whether you curse heaven because you are unsatisfied or choose to regard non-satisfaction as the real meaning of pleasure; the ambiguity is due to a slight variation of attitude in relation

188

to the first factor. And this carefully cultivated suffering came to his aid again in the form of self-punishment when he wanted to take his revenge on Good by an unfulfilled transcendence while at the same time it enabled him to assert his otherness in the most categorical fashion. But between extreme self-affirmation and ultimate self-negation there was once again not the slightest difference. For when he denied himself completely he thought of killing himself. Now with Baudelaire suicide was nothing but an aspiration towards the absolute void. When he imagined that he was going to destroy himself, he wanted to cause the disappearance in himself of the *nature* which he identified with the present and with the limbo of consciousness. He asked from the idea of suicide this small service, this bagatelle which would enable him to regard his life as irremediable and complete, as an eternal destiny or, if one prefers it, as a past which was closed. Above all he saw in the act of putting an end to his life the ultimate recovery of his being. It was suicide which would draw the line; it was, finally, suicide which by bringing his life to a stop would transform it into an *essence* which would be at once given for ever and for ever created by himself. In this way he would free himself once and for all from the intolerable feeling of being *one too many* in the world. There was only one thing. In order to enjoy the results of his suicide, it was obviously essential that he should survive it. That is why Baudelaire chose to set up as a *survivor*. And if he did not kill himself at a single blow, at any rate he behaved in such a way that each of his actions was the symbolical equivalent of a suicide that he couldn't commit. Fri-

189

gidity, impotence, sterility, absense of generosity, refusal to serve, sin—we see once again that there were so many equivalents of suicide. For Baudelaire, to assert himself meant in effect to posit himself as a pure inactive essence, that is to say, to posit himself at bottom as a memory (*mémoire*); and to deny himself meant to wish once for all to be nothing but the unalterable chain of his memories (*Souvenirs*). And poetic creation, which he preferred to every form of action, was associated for him with the suicide which he never ceased to brood over. Poetry attracted him in the first place because it allowed him to exercise his freedom without any danger; but it attracted him chiefly because it was removed from every form of *gift,* for the idea of gift inspired him with horror. When he wrote a poem he thought that he was giving people nothing or at least that he was only giving them a useless object. He did not serve; he remained greedy and shut up in himself; he did not compromise himself in his creation. At the same time the discipline of rhythm and versification forced him to pursue in this field the *ascesis* which he practised by his taste in clothes and his dandyism. He imposed a form on his feelings as he had imposed a form on his body and his movements. Baudelaire's poems have a dandyism of their own. Finally, the object which he produced was only an image of himself, a restoration in the present of his memory which offered the appearance of a synthesis of being and existence. And since he was more than half engaged in it, when he tried to appropriate it to himself he did not succeed completely; he remained unsatisfied. Thus the object of desire was paired off with the desire in order to form in the end this rigid, perverse, unsatisfied totality which was none other than Baudelaire himself. As we can see, self-negation 'passes into' self-affirmation, as it does in the Hegelian dialectic; suicide becomes a method of perpetuating oneself; suffering—Baudelaire's famous suffering—has the same intimate structure as pleasure; poetic creation is related to sterility. All these passing forms, all these daily attitudes melt into one another, appear, disappear and reappear when one imagined oneself farthest from them. They are only modulations of a great primitive theme which they reproduce with different tonalities.

We know the theme which we have not lost sight of for a moment. It is Baudelaire's initial choice of himself. He chose to *exist* for himself as he *was* for others. He wanted his freedom to appear to himself like a 'nature'; and he wanted this 'nature' which others discovered in him to appear to them like the very emanation of his freedom. From that point everything becomes clear. We understand now that this wretched life, which seemed to be going to rack and ruin, was carefully planned by him. It was he who transformed it into a survival; he who encumbered it from the start with that vast collection of bric-à-brac—the negress, debts, pox, family council—which embarrassed him to the very end and to the very end forced him to move backwards into the future. It was he who invented the calm, beautiful women, Marie Daubrun and the Présidente, who moved through his years of boredom. It was he who carefully delimited the geography of his existence by deciding to drag his miseries around with him in a great city and by refusing all real changes of scene so that he was better able to continue his imaginary escapes in his own room. It was he who replaced voyages by removals and simulated flight from himself by perpetually changing his place of residence and who, when mortally sick, only consented to leave Paris to go to another city which was a caricature of it. It was he again who brought about his partial failure as a writer and chose that brilliant and precarious isolation in the world of letters. It seems that in this life which was so closed and narrow, an accident or the intervention of chance would have enabled one to breathe, would have given a respite to the *heautontimoroumenos*. But we should look in vain for a single circumstance for which he was not fully and consciously responsible. Every event was a reflection of that indecomposable totality which he was from the first to the last day of his life. He refused experience. Nothing came from outside to change him and he learned nothing. General Aupick's death scarcely altered his relations with his mother. For the rest, his story is the story of a very slow, very painful decomposition. Such he was at the age of twenty; such we shall find him on the eve of his death. He is simply gloomier, more nervous, less alive, while of his talent and his admirable intelligence nothing remains except memories. And such no doubt was his singularity, that 'difference' which he sought until death and which was only visible to others. He was an experiment in a retort, something like the *homunculus* in the Second Part of *Faust;* and the quasi-abstract circumstances of the experiment enabled him to bear witness with unequalled éclat to this truth—the free choice which a man makes of himself is completely identified with what is called his destiny.